Coaching Youth Baseball the Ripken Way

Cal Ripken, Jr.
Bill Ripken

with Scott Lowe

HUMAN
KINETICS

Library of Congress Cataloging-in-Publication Data

Ripken, Cal, 1960-
  Coaching youth baseball the Ripken way / Cal Ripken, Jr., Bill Ripken;
with Scott Lowe.
    p. cm.
  Includes index.
  ISBN-13: 978-0-7360-6782-9 (soft cover)
  ISBN-10: 0-7360-6782-5 (soft cover)
  1. Youth league baseball--Coaching. 2. Baseball for
children--Training. I. Ripken, Bill. II. Lowe, Scott, 1969- III. Title.

  GV880.65.R56 2007
  796.357'62--dc22   2006029707

ISBN-10: 0-7360-6782-5
ISBN-13: 978-0-7360-6782-9

The Web addresses cited in this text were current as of November 15th, 2006, unless otherwise noted.

Acquisitions Editor: Jason Muzinic; **Developmental Editor:** Cynthia McEntire; **Assistant Editor:** Scott Hawkins; **Copyeditor:** John Wentworth; **Proofreader:** Jim Burns; **Indexer:** Dan Connolly; **Graphic Designer:** Nancy Rasmus; **Graphic Artists:** Kim McFarland, Tara Welsch, and Sandra Meier; **Photo Manager:** Brenda Williams; **Cover Designer:** Keith Blomberg; **Photographer (cover):** Bill Wood; **Photographer (interior):** Brenda Williams; **Art Manager:** Kelly Hendren; **Illustrator:** Al Wilborn; **Printer:** Sheridan Books

We thank Ripken Baseball, Inc. and the Ripken Baseball Academy in Aberdeen, Maryland, for assistance in providing the location for the photo shoot for this book.

Human Kinetics books are available at special discounts for bulk purchase. Special editions or book excerpts can also be created to specification. For details, contact the Special Sales Manager at Human Kinetics.

Printed in the United States of America   10 9 8 7

The paper in this book is certified under a sustainable forestry program.

Human Kinetics
Web site: www.HumanKinetics.com

United States: Human Kinetics
P.O. Box 5076
Champaign, IL 61825-5076
800-747-4457
e-mail: humank@hkusa.com

Canada: Human Kinetics
475 Devonshire Road, Unit 100
Windsor, ON N8Y 2L5
800-465-7301 (in Canada only)
e-mail: info@hkcanada.com

Europe: Human Kinetics
107 Bradford Road
Stanningley
Leeds LS28 6AT, United Kingdom
+44 (0)113 255 5665
e-mail: hk@hkeurope.com

Australia: Human Kinetics
57A Price Avenue
Lower Mitcham, South Australia 5062
08 8372 0999
e-mail: info@hkaustralia.com

New Zealand: Human Kinetics
P.O. Box 80
Torrens Park, South Australia 5062
0800 222 062
e-mail: info@hknewzealand.com

Coaching Youth Baseball the Ripken Way

Contents

PART I   Coaching the Ripken Way

PART II   Teaching the Ripken Way

PART III Practicing the Ripken Way

Foreword

Jim Leyland

I had the good fortune to manage against Cal Ripken, Sr., back in 1974 in the Southern League. To this day I believe that he was one of the best fundamental baseball teachers I have ever been around.

Cal Sr. was one of my all-time favorite baseball guys. He got a reputation for being a no-nonsense person, and some people today might call him "old school." I don't buy any of that. Cal Ripken, Sr., stood for doing things the right way, plain and simple. It wasn't his way, or the Oriole Way, or the Ripken Way. It was the right way, and to me that's what was most impressive about him. He was an incredible tutor who made a lasting impression on a lot of big league players.

The impact that Cal Sr. had on his sons, Cal Jr. and Billy, has been obvious since the day they both stepped on a big league field for the first time. I have been around both of them quite a bit. I coached third base in the American League while Cal was in his prime and even coached against him during the playoffs in 1983. I have spoken to them on many occasions and enjoyed their insights about the game. Both are very talented to have played at the highest level for so many years, but the one thing that always stuck out in my mind was the way that they loved baseball and respected the game as well as the people who played it. Everyone wants to talk about all the home runs and the records, but what I appreciate most about them is their love for the game, their respect for the game, and the way they respect their dad's teachings. It's very touching.

What the Ripken brothers are doing, in my mind, is simply continuing their dad's tradition of teaching the sport the right way, and that's very impressive. They have decided, in the aftermath of all the information that their dad passed down to them, to teach kids the same love and respect for the game that they learned from him. Their goal is to show kids how to play the right way and how to approach the sport the way that they were taught.

Any time that our pastime can be associated with the Ripkens, it gives our sport instant credibility. While the game seems to be thriving at the Major League level, it has lost some ground at the youth level to sports such as soccer, basketball, and football. Cal and Billy Ripken have found another way to give back to the game that their dad taught them to love, and hopefully that will help put our pastime back on the map.

In this book you'll read about the Ripken Way. Well, you might as well call it the *Right Way*. The right way to play, and the right way to teach. There are no gimmicks. It's a method that follows a very simple formula and provides a solid foundation. The programs that Cal and Billy run are not five-minute autograph sessions. Kids who go to their camps are going to get an experience that will stick with them forever. For any kid to be able to get instruction from Cal and Billy Ripken, I mean real instruction and attention, and not take advantage of that opportunity would be foolish.

I'd have to say the same about any coaches who don't read this book. When it comes to baseball instruction, we are always looking for the best information to help us develop a better understanding of the game. One of Cal's former managers once said, "It's what you learn after you know it all that counts." Some people might say that I know everything there is to know about baseball, but those of us who make our living in the game know otherwise. You never stop learning about the game. If you do, there's a good chance that you won't be making your living in baseball for very long.

I guarantee you that I can learn something from a family that has accumulated 80 years of experience in professional baseball. That's why I'm reading this book. It's an honor to be associated with the Ripkens. I'm thrilled that they have asked me to express my thoughts to you here. Take advantage of this opportunity to learn from one of baseball's all-time great families. I wish you the best of luck as you pass along Cal and Billy's lessons to the players on your team.

Introduction: The Ripken Way

Several years ago we decided that we wanted to influence the game of baseball at the grassroots level. We started a company, Ripken Baseball, with a specific mission: to grow the game of baseball worldwide the Ripken Way. We began by attempting to influence youth players directly. The Babe Ruth League named its 12-and-under division, which had more than 600,000 players at the time, Cal Ripken Baseball, and we began running youth baseball camps all over the country.

As we continued running camps and became more involved in the 12-and-under Cal Ripken World Series, we began taking the pulse of youth baseball. It didn't take long for us to realize that there was a greater opportunity to reach more youth players in a positive manner by arming their coaches with information through clinics, books, and videos. In addition to our youth camps that host more than 1,500 kids annually, we have been conducting all-day coaching clinics in venues around the country since 2002. We have produced an instructional CD-ROM, and our instructional book, *Play Baseball the Ripken Way*, was released in April 2004. In January of 2005, we released a series of instructional DVDs covering pitching, hitting, and defense. As we have been developing these programs, the Cal Ripken Division of Babe Ruth Baseball has been the only national youth baseball organization to grow each year since 1999. In addition, we have started a free e-mail newsletter specifically for youth baseball coaches called *Coach's Clipboard* (available at **www.ripkenbaseball.com/cc**) with the goal of reaching 100,000 subscribers. Our ultimate ambition is to unite all amateur baseball coaches through a coaching education or certification program that operates across all leagues and all age groups. That program should be in place for Babe Ruth League coaches by the time this book is released.

Introducing the Ripken Way

Baseball instruction has been a part of our family for as long as any of us can remember. For 37 years our dad, Cal Ripken, Sr., was a player, coach, and manager in the Baltimore Orioles' organization. As kids we had the good fortune of being around the ballpark almost every day and the better fortune of learning the game from our dad almost every day. Dad developed instructional manuals for players and coaches that were used at all levels of the Orioles' organization during a period of time when Baltimore was the most respected franchise in the game. Those manuals formed the basis of what became known as the Oriole way. Later, because of Dad's efforts at the big league level, as well as the success that we had as Major League players, many people began referring to these methods as the Ripken Way.

Since Dad passed away in 1999, we have put a great deal of thought into exactly what the Ripken Way means in relation to our instructional philosophies. We've thought about all the lessons Dad taught us, lessons that helped us become better ballplayers and better people, as well as everything we learned during our combined 33 years in the big leagues. All the while we kept one eye focused on the game of baseball and what's necessary to motivate more kids to play the game and make sure that they keep on playing the game. Here is what we have adopted as the Ripken Way pertaining to baseball instruction.

Keep It Simple

As Dad used to say, baseball is a simple game played with bats, balls, and people. No matter the level at which you play, the team that throws, catches, and hits best wins. Even the most complicated and advanced plays in baseball tend to be combinations of the simplest fundamentals. Consider a double play, for example. Broken down into its simplest form, a double play is nothing more than a catch, a throw, a catch, a throw, and a catch.

Keeping drills and instruction simple allows players at the youngest ages to build a solid fundamental base without experiencing the frustration of being unable to accomplish the tasks being taught. For the more advanced players it helps to fine tune the fundamentals that are necessary to compete at the highest levels. You can't learn to make difficult plays by practicing difficult plays. Perfecting the fundamentals allows players to adapt to any situation that may arise on the field. Once that's accomplished, the spectacular and more complicated plays start occurring with greater regularity.

Explain Why

If we, as coaches or instructors, can't explain why players should do something a certain way, we lose our credibility. Even more important, if we can't explain why we do things the way we do, a young player is likely to fall back on old habits that may be incorrect. "Why?" is a young person's favorite question. We believe in presenting certain concepts to even the youngest players that they may not grasp entirely the first time, but our ability to explain *why* will make sense to them, and they'll continue to attempt to complete a drill or play the way we prefer. At some point down the road, a situation is going to arise or a play is going to develop, and they're going to naturally be able to execute it. They'll then think back and remember that they learned that from the Ripkens.

Celebrate the Individual

Every player, young or old, brings a certain style or flair to the game. We don't want to stifle that. In fact, we want to encourage and celebrate it. Kids are attracted to the style and flair that they see on the basketball court and on the football field, so what's wrong with seeing it on the baseball diamond as well? As long as they're following certain fundamental approaches, we want the players we teach to perform within their own comfort zones.

Make It Fun

Baseball is a *game*. We should never lose sight of that. Whether we're dealing with 8-year-olds or 22-year-olds, baseball should be fun. When it ceases to be fun, the sport loses participants. Games, by their nature, are fun. But, believe it or not, by simply turning simple drills into contests or coming up with crazy ways of teaching (so that kids aren't even aware that they're learning), we can make practices even more fun than the games. That's when we begin developing baseball players and fans for life.

As you can see, we've already put a great deal of thought into youth baseball instruction and what's needed to return the game to the status it once enjoyed in our sporting landscape. In some ways we've learned through trial and error. But after 33 years of playing at the highest level, countless more years being taught by Dad and hanging around professional ballparks, and teaching thousands of kids in more than 50 cities through our brand of instruction, we feel pretty confident that what we have to offer can really help make coaching easier, more fun, and more rewarding.

Through baseball camps and clinics, we have reached thousands of players and youth coaches with the principles of the Ripken Way.

Although we have begun to make a real impact on baseball at the grassroots level, there's still a great deal of work to be done. We realize that most of the people coaching baseball are volunteering their valuable free time in hopes of creating a memorable experience for a group of eager young players. This book is designed to help make that experience easier and more enjoyable for coaches and players alike.

Implementing the Ripken Way

Not too long ago coaches were considered teachers first and foremost. Even at the college level, most coaches had some sort of teaching background, either practical experience in the classroom or a college degree in education. Coaches of professional sports franchises, of course, have always been focused on winning first. But, even at that level, the best coaches are those who can successfully teach an effective system and communicate well with their players and assistant coaches.

Because of the economics of sport in today's society, the pressure to win at the top levels has become enormous, and just like with almost everything else in our culture, that pressure starts to trickle down to the lower levels. Some of the great coaches and teachers of our time lose their jobs after one subpar season. Just about every professional contest in every sport is televised these days. Local and national networks pay millions, even billions, of dollars for the rights to televise events. More and more college sporting events are televised every year. Football bowl game payouts are well into the millions of dollars. CBS pays more than a billion dollars for the rights to televise the NCAA basketball tournament. Every decision by a coach in every contest is studied and analyzed by the media. Fans and analysts flood local sports talk radio shows with their opinions. In some regions, this type of public pressure has filtered down to the high school level. Even at the lower levels—take AAU basketball, for instance—there is pressure to win or attract a certain caliber of player so that money or products can be obtained from one of the big-time shoe or sporting goods companies.

Similar pressures, to a lesser degree, seem to have appeared within youth sports as well. In baseball, travel teams have become more and more popular, with kids as young as 8 years old playing 35 or more games each summer. These teams compete for national rankings and various national or "world series" championships. Parents put pressure on the coaches to play the right players, usually their kids, and to make the right moves to win as many games as possible. Young players are sitting on the bench just so they can say they play on a travel team. Parents who are upset with how their kids' teams are being handled decide to simply start their own travel programs with the primary goal of being better than the team they just left.

Participation in the sport of baseball has been declining consistently for more than a decade. The win-at-all-costs mentality, especially at the youngest ages, is not helping the situation. The pressure and number of games can cause players to burn out at younger and younger ages. Some of these players will grow up and transfer this type of approach to their children at even younger ages. The game gets serious fast enough. There's no reason to rush the process. If we handle the players correctly at the youngest levels, we'll create lifelong baseball players, fans, and coaches—that's the key to cultivating this wonderful game.

Certainly, the win-at-all-cost mentality doesn't exist throughout youth sports. There are thousands of well-intentioned volunteer coaches who want only to create a positive experience for all of their players. They want the kids to have fun and learn something—a very simple formula. Unfortunately, in baseball, it seems that many of the volunteer coaches either don't have the knowledge or the resources to make the game as fun as it should be. This is not their fault.

Many times, parents volunteer to coach out of the kindness of their hearts because no one else will step up to do the job. They might have more than one child playing on different teams, they have full-time jobs, they volunteer to assist or have responsibilities with other organizations, they have hobbies and interests that all of us need to strike a happy balance in our lives, and they have to worry about the general, everyday upkeep of their homes. The bottom line is that most of us have a lot of responsibilities. Usually, when people decide to volunteer to coach a team, they have the best intentions. They want the experience to be positive, for their own children, of course, and for everyone else involved. The problem is that day-to-day life and its responsibilities compete for the volunteer's time and attention. Planning practices and communicating with parents takes time and a certain amount of knowledge. Most volunteers don't have the free time to search the Internet or go to the library to read about how they can make the athletic experience as fulfilling as possible for their players. We understand this and have attempted to solve the problem as far as baseball is concerned by developing an easy-to-read coaching book that serves as a quick reference for youth coaches of any age group.

In this book we break down everything by age. What's fun and interesting for a 5-year-old can be boring for an 8-year-old. You can't spend an entire practice teaching a bunch of 7-year-olds how to defend in bunt situations, and you can't have a group of 12-year-olds who spend half of every practice running the bases. Baseball is a simple game, and the skills of throwing, hitting, and catching need to be stressed across all age groups. But the methods used to teach those skills, the window of attention that's available to teach them, and the concepts of understanding rules and team play that can be absorbed vary considerably across age groups.

In this book you'll find five goals that baseball coaches should strive to accomplish at various age groups. We break the groups into ages 4 to 6, 7 to 9, 10 to 12, 13 to 14, and 15 and up. As we have said, we prefer to keep things simple. Setting simple, attainable goals allows coaches to develop an easy formula for creating effective and fun practices. It allows them to use their time efficiently and ensure an enjoyable experience for their teams.

Keeping things simple doesn't mean that our philosophies and teachings are too basic for more advanced players or that they lack substance. Remember what our dad used to say: "Baseball is a simple game played with bats, balls, and people." That really sums it up. Derek Jeter catches a ground ball and throws it to first the same way that an 8-year-old should. The teams that throw and catch the best are generally the most successful. Hitting a baseball is difficult enough without giving a young player too much information to think about when he or she is standing at home plate. There are no shortcuts to becoming a better baseball player. Players must practice the basic fundamentals until they become second nature. At that point the more complicated and difficult plays occur automatically.

But we're getting a bit ahead of ourselves. The rest of the book will be dedicated to setting and attaining goals and developing effective and enjoyable practices for all ages. First we need to discuss the responsibilities that coaches of all age groups share.

Baseball is the same game for an 8-year-old as it is for a 22-year-old. We've said it before, and we'll say it over and over again. If we watch two teams warm up before a game, more times than not we can tell which team will win by watching them play catch. The team that plays catch best is the team that generally wins the game. This sounds like an oversimplification, but you might be surprised how many times it actually works out that way. The players who make the travel teams play catch better than the players who play on recreational teams. The players who play high school ball play catch better than the players who play on the travel teams. The players who play on college teams play catch better than high school players. The players who play minor league ball play catch better than the college players. And the big league players play catch best of all. Take a look at the daily Major League box scores in your newspaper or on the Internet and you'll see how many times the team that makes the fewest errors wins. You might be amazed. It really is that simple. Keep that in mind. This book is designed to be very simple, just like the game of baseball.

If you take the basic plans that we lay out for you here, incorporate the drills, involve other parents, take the time to be organized, and always try to think of creative ways to make the drills and teachings fun, you'll find that the progress you make with your team and the excitement your players show for the game of baseball will turn coaching into a very rewarding experience. Who knows, maybe you'll become a coach for life. Either way you'll be doing the kids you're teaching and the game of baseball a great service.

We hope that you enjoy this book and use it to make your life as a coach easier and your players' experiences more fulfilling. Please check our Web site at **www.ripkenbaseball.com** and consider subscribing to our free *Coach's Clipboard* newsletter (**www.ripkenbaseball.com/cc**) to receive updates and articles from us. E-mail us about what works and what doesn't. Let us know when you come up with creative drills that are successful in teaching the Ripken Way. We'll be happy to post them on our site and give you full credit. It doesn't matter to us where the ideas come from as long as they're good for the game and for our kids. We hope that your experience as a youth baseball coach is rewarding and enjoyable. Now it's time to play ball!

Key to Diagrams

Path of ball	------>
Path of player (running)	——>
CH	Coach
F	Fungo hitter
B	Batter
C	Catcher
P	Pitcher
R	Runner
ⓡ	Relay/cutoff man
X	Any player
1B	First baseman
2B	Second baseman
3B	Third baseman
SS	Shortstop
CF	Center fielder
RF	Right fielder
LF	Left fielder
Δ	Cone
■	Pitching machine
L	L-screen
⊔	Bucket of balls

PART I

Coaching the Ripken Way

1

Responsibilities of Coaching

Baseball gets serious fast enough. As coaches, we need to recognize this and do our best not to put too much pressure on young, developing baseball players. These days it's not uncommon to see 8-, 9-, and 10-year-old kids playing 40 or more baseball games in a summer for their local travel teams. In some ways this is great. Youth players today have opportunities to play baseball that we never had. If the kids wake up every day and all they talk about is that day's game or practice—if they're truly excited to get out on the baseball field that often without being pushed—then, by all means, let them have at it.

The truth of the matter, however, is that for most kids that's too much baseball. When kids get to be 11 or 12 years old, they begin forming their own likes and dislikes. Kids at this age start making their own decisions on what they want to do. If they don't want to play that many games, they won't; it's as simple as that. Younger children are not so independent in their thinking, however. Most of them still want to do what makes mom or dad happy. So, the danger is that there will be kids who really do enjoy the game of baseball on a recreational level and will keep going out there to play on a travel team every day because it's what their parents want. At some point, usually when they turn 11 or 12, these kids will get sick of the sport and look for other ways to spend their recreational time. This is dangerous for the future of baseball.

You also have the other extreme, which is just as dangerous. Many kids enjoy baseball or are at least curious about the sport. They want to be part of a team and to learn and enjoy the game in a structured environment. We call these kids recreational or in-house players. However, if you look at these kids as the seeds representing the future of the game, it's very important to nurture them properly, just as you would water the grass seed in your front yard or the seeds for the flowers you've planted in your garden.

Children don't mature at the same rate physically. Plus their interest levels and attention spans vary considerably from age group to age group. If a player is interested in baseball at a very young age but is not as physically prepared to play as some of his or her peers, that player's interests and needs must be considered. If that player has a positive experience, he or she is likely to stick with the sport. At some point he or she is going to mature and might turn into a heck of a ballplayer. If he or she is neglected or has an otherwise negative experience early on, the sport of baseball loses out on a potential superstar or, at the very least, a potential lifelong fan. Neither of these outcomes is good for the game.

Similarly, if a player is only moderately interested in the sport, it's important that his or her interest be cultivated and maintained. There are a lot of activities competing for the attention of the young people in this country. If I'm an active 10-year-old and can play basketball, baseball, football, or soccer, I'm probably going to give them all a try to find out which ones I like. Initial experiences and impressions significantly influence how a child feels about something. If football practice is more exciting than baseball practice, I'm probably going to make sure I make it to football practice every time. I'll go to baseball practice when I feel like it or if it fits into my schedule.

With all this in mind, it's easy to see that youth baseball coaches— most of them volunteers trying to balance their own work and family lives with coaching—play an enormous role in shaping a child's on-field experience. Almost all male adults played baseball at some point in their lives. It's one game that everyone seems to think they know something about. So, when our kids decide to play T-ball or baseball, we feel confident that we can get out there for a few hours a week and make a positive impact by coaching their teams.

Unfortunately, it's not that simple. Baseball is a game that lends itself to some standing around. A lot of the strategy and thinking involved in baseball takes place in between the actual game action. As we get older, the strategic part of the game becomes very appealing to us.

Young kids need to be kept engaged and active in practice or they become easily distracted.

Younger kids are not built that way, however. Attention spans are short at the younger ages, and energy levels are high. If these factors aren't considered by the youth baseball or T-ball coach, their players' earliest experiences can be negative.

So, as you can see, there's a fine line to walk as a youth baseball coach. Again, think of the kids as seeds that need to be nurtured. Every seed is a little bit different and needs its own personal attention. You're not going to treat grass seed the same way you treat a pumpkin seed or a geranium seed. If you treat them all the same way, some will grow and others will die. Likewise, if you try to handle every kid at every age the same way, you're going to kill some of the kids' interest along the way, and participation will decrease.

Motor skill development is age-specific. Sure, you're going to find some advanced 5-year-olds who can catch thrown and hit balls pretty regularly. But, for most kids that age, catching is one of the hardest skills to develop. As coaches, we need to be able to cater to the needs of the kid who can't catch one ball and still make baseball fun and exciting for the kid who can. It's a difficult balance but one that's important to understand at all age levels.

Be an Effective Communicator

One of the most frequent excuses we hear from coaches is that other parents aren't willing to help, that it's impossible to run effective practices or coach effectively when flying solo. We feel that many times this is a simple issue of communication. A meeting with the team's parents before the season and an open line of communication during the season can eliminate this problem.

Before the season begins, the coach should hold a meeting with all team parents. In this meeting the coach should discuss what he or she hopes to accomplish with the team during the season. These plans should be in line with the age-appropriate goals we'll get to later in this book. It's also important for the coach to stress that to run efficient, fun, and effective practices and to make the experience as enjoyable as possible for the kids, parental assistance is needed.

Usually, a coach will ask for one or two volunteers to serve as assistant coaches. Trying to find one or two more people with the free time to be at every practice can be quite a challenge. What generally happens is that assistants volunteer and have good intentions, but because they're not head coaches, they find it easier to miss a practice or a game when another commitment intrudes.

A more effective way to enlist support and ensure proper staffing of all practices is to explain that to run great practices and make the experience as fun as possible for the kids, a certain level of support is needed. Explain the elements of a good practice—small groups or stations, a variety of activities, organization, and so on—and how these elements will benefit their kids. If the coach is organized and communicates well, many parents will see the value of his or her plan and try to help.

At this point the coach should feel comfortable asking each parent to serve as a volunteer assistant for one or two weeks during the season while encouraging parents to come out and assist whenever they have free time. Or, alternatively, a coach could ask for two different parents to help at each practice and game.

Alternatives to Trying Out

Cal Ripken, Jr.

I don't remember really trying out for a baseball team until I reached high school. By "trying out" I mean being awarded a spot on a team because of performance or merit. These days I hear about kids as young as the age of 7 trying out for teams. I also have heard of situations in which 35 players have tried out for a single open spot on a travel team.

Any time players try out for a team that is being chosen based on merit, there is going to be rejection. Being cut from a team, or rejected, can be a devastating experience for young players who just don't have the mental maturity to be able to handle that type of experience the way a young adult or an adult can.

When a young player goes into a situation in which he or she knows that a certain level of performance is necessary to be chosen for a team, it can be very stressful. Likewise, kids who know that they are going to an evaluation of any kind often freeze up and are unable to perform up to their capabilities. The challenge is for youth leagues and teams to find a way to match up players of similar skill levels and place them in appropriate programs.

I remember signing up for baseball as a kid and being placed on a team. Today it seems as though most kids register to play baseball and then go to a tryout or evaluation of some sort. The goal of the evaluation is to place a diverse group of kids from the same age group on teams in such a way that the league is balanced. While this is a noble objective, the term "evaluation" can be intimidating to young players and hinder their performance.

It seems to me that a better idea would be to bring all the players who have signed up to play baseball from several age groups together for an instructional clinic. This clinic could take place over the course of three mornings or three evenings, allowing coaches and other instructors to teach the players the basic fundamentals of the game. At the same time the coaches would have an opportunity to evaluate the players without them knowing it.

This format would give coaches a truer sense of each player's skill level, because the kids would be performing in a depressurized environment. In addition, players of lower abilities and lesser experience would have an opportunity to learn the game's fundamentals

(continued)

(continued)

and understand what they need to do to get better. Parents wouldn't decide if their kids were too good for a certain age group, because coaches would be able to match players more accurately based on their ability levels. The higher-skilled players could be invited to play on a travel team if they were interested in a more competitive atmosphere.

A clinic format instead of tryouts or evaluations provides coaches with an opportunity to distribute the talent more evenly and provides players with some instruction and drills to help them improve. This format eliminates the possibility that a young athlete's first exposure to the game of baseball might result in rejection and turn him or her off to the sport. A clinic atmosphere also makes it more likely for players of similar skill levels to be grouped together, which would help ensure a positive experience for more kids for the duration of the season. Creating more positive experiences for more young players is what's going to help us expand the popularity of the game of baseball.

In many youth leagues there will be no more than one practice and two games per week, so this is really not much to ask. The more organized the coach is and the more effectively he or she communicates in this meeting, the easier it will be to get additional help.

Developing an e-mail list and sending out a short practice plan to all players and parents, and sending out the team's batting order for the next game the night before, also makes parents aware that the coach is organized and concerned. If you keep people informed, the chances of enlisting their support on the field increases. Coaches should always be accessible to parents who have questions, and questions should be answered in a timely and polite manner, no matter the circumstances.

This system might not be appropriate for older age groups or travel teams. Generally, as players get older or more advanced, a group of coaches emerges to guide the team from year to year. Of course, at the high school level, head and assistant coaches are designated by the school. However, opening the lines of communication with the parents before and during the season is essential for all coaches. For coaches of older and more advanced teams, good communication will help parents understand and appreciate the time commitment made by the coach and will eliminate some of the questioning that often goes on during a season and can be demoralizing and frustrating to a coach.

Create a Safe, Enjoyable Environment

When parents trust their kids with another adult, they want to be sure that their children are going to have fun and be properly supervised. It is imperative that coaches design their practices so that there is adequate supervision. For example, if only one volunteer assistant shows up to help the coach out for a particular practice, it doesn't make sense to divide the team into three groups. That means one of the groups would be unsupervised. Unsupervised groups generally don't accomplish what they are supposed to, and the lack of adult supervision can lead to injuries. As players get older there are drills and tasks that they can handle on their own. But even at the high school level, practices are more efficient and productive when there is a coach assigned to each specific group or drill.

Baseball is a game and should be treated as such at all levels. Sure, winning becomes more important as players get older and better, but if we are not dealing with professional athletes, the lessons to be learned through playing the game and the positives of being part of a team have a much bigger impact on the lives of those involved than winning or

For safe practices, enlist the help of other coaches. All players need to be supervised properly.

losing ever will. Those concepts should be stressed in hopes of making the experience less stressful and more enjoyable at all levels.

By using this book and understanding the types of practices and drills that are appropriate for specific ages, coaches can ensure their practices are enjoyable. Baseball games are always fun for kids, but there's no reason that practice can't be just as enjoyable. As we said earlier, baseball is a game that includes a good deal of standing around. Practices should be created with an eye toward eliminating the standing around. Small groups moving from station to station every few minutes will help kids maintain their attention and excitement level.

Understanding what skills certain age groups are capable of handling will keep the frustration level to a minimum. Getting creative by devising games and contests that help players learn skills will increase the level of enjoyment. We'll discuss all these concepts later in the book.

We recommend that all coaches be safety, first aid, and CPR certified. However, until this is required by all youth baseball organizations, it's impractical to think that everyone will have the time or desire to obtain those certifications. It's important, however, to have a stocked medical kit on hand at all times and to be aware of the particular league or organization's safety, emergency, and lightning policies. Another good idea is to be aware of any parents on the team who might work in medical fields or be safety, first aid, or CPR certified. This knowledge can be invaluable in emergency situations.

Coaches must also make sure that all required protective equipment—protective cup, catcher's gear, batting helmets, and so on—is worn by players at the proper times and that the protective equipment fits correctly and is in good working condition. Helmets should be worn by all players who are at a hitting station and by all players who are running the bases.

Be a Role Model

Just as kids imitate their parents and teachers, they're going to take cues from their coaches when it comes to how they act on the baseball diamond. A coach's attitude and behavior sets the tone for the atmosphere surrounding a team. If a coach gets visibly frustrated with his players, the higher-skilled players on the team are more likely to get frustrated with the lower-skilled players. The lower-skilled players might get easily frustrated with themselves and not enjoy the sport.

Similarly, a coach who yells at umpires is going to promote that type of behavior within his or her team and among the team's supporters. At the youngest levels, this may translate into players who grow up thinking that abusing umpires verbally is part of the game. At the older and more advanced levels, this type of behavior could create an ugly atmosphere that surrounds a team as coaches, parents, and supporters get a reputation for being abusive toward umpires.

Coaches at all levels should be positive and upbeat when dealing with their teams. If a coach is consistently negative, players are going to dread coming to practice. Even young players are very observant. If it looks as if the coach does not enjoy being there, why would the players enjoy being there? Coaches should *never* single out a player about a mistake in front of everyone on the field. That type of embarrassment can lead to a negative experience that may diminish a young player's desire to play the game.

A player who has made a mistake on the field already is upset. He or she is worrying about the next play or what mom is thinking. At that particular time, a verbal lesson or reminder from the coach is not going to be absorbed. Always wait for an opportunity to discuss the situation with the player in private. We like to call this a "teachable moment." Then, at the next practice, you can devise a drill to re-create the situation without singling out a particular player.

The bottom line is that if the coach creates an environment of pressure, shouts, and complaints, the team will take on that type of personality. When that occurs, a certain percentage of young players and parents are going to be turned off by the game.

Be Organized

Kids are very perceptive, often even more so than parents. If a coach is coming to practice without a plan and is basically flying by the seat of his or her pants, that will be evident to the kids. Of course parents will pick up on this, too. By spending a few minutes the day before developing a practice plan (and preferably e-mailing the plan to all players and parents), the coach will show everyone that he or she really cares about creating the best possible experience for all who are involved. In addition, a well-organized practice will eliminate any down time or standing around. If the coach can create a schedule and stick with it, the kids should move from one activity to another quickly, which will ensure that they maintain their attention and stay energized.

Adhere to the Ripken Way

As discussed in the introduction to this book, after years of instructing thousands of youth baseball players, we have developed what we call the Ripken Way. By sticking to our philosophy—keep it simple, explain why, celebrate the individual, and make it fun—at all times, you should find it relatively easy to adhere to the responsibilities discussed in this chapter. If the environment you create is fun, safe, and educational, you're off to a great start.

2

Realities of Coaching

Coaching youth sports can be one of the most rewarding experiences imaginable. It can also be one of the most frustrating. For the most part, once everything is said and done, the positive memories outweigh the negative. Above all else you'll remember the smiles on the kids' faces and the progress that they made. But, at times, when you find yourself muddling through the more difficult situations, seeing that light at the end of the tunnel can be difficult.

Most coaches in our country are volunteers, so when you find yourself balancing your professional life, your home life, and your baseball team, trying times can make you question your decision to coach. Even coaches who are fortunate enough to get paid for their time usually don't make much money, so when some of the realities of coaching set in—such as parental meddling and questioning, parental pressure to win, the difficulties of balancing your personal life with games and practices, keeping the kids happy, avoiding burnout, and so on—as with anything, it can be easier to just throw up your hands and walk away.

Unfortunately, these realities, paired with a lack of resources available to coaches, cause our sport to lose many potentially excellent coaches and other established, successful coaches each year. We are hoping that this book can arm amateur baseball coaches with enough

13

information to make the coaching experience as smooth and enjoyable as possible. If you've decided to dedicate some of your valuable free time to this game that we love so much, we want to give you what you need to be successful and keep you involved in the sport for a long time.

One of the realities we face in life is that it's impossible to please everyone all the time. Coaching is the same way. If coaches understand and accept that going in, dealing with the obstacles and issues that present themselves should be easier. Your ultimate goal should be to do your job the right way and do it for the right reasons. If you are organized and honest, communicate well, and keep the best interests of the kids foremost in your mind, everything should work out fine. If you approach coaching in this manner, you might run into some difficult situations along the way, but chances are good that you'll make as many people happy as humanly possible. At the very least you'll be able to look in the mirror and know that you approached it the right way.

What follows are some of the realities that all coaches face and some thoughts about how to cope with them.

Dealing With Parental Pressures

As we mentioned in chapter 1, being an effective communicator is one of the key responsibilities for a coach. Perhaps the most important avenue of communication for coaches—from the youngest ages all the way up through the college level—is the one you establish with the parents of your players.

We recommend that you hold a preseason meeting with parents during which you explain your philosophies about teaching, winning and losing, and playing time. Discuss your practice philosophy and the level of commitment you expect from parents and players. Present your goals for the team. Taking this positive first step should answer most of the parents' initial questions and eliminate at least some of the second guessing that occurs during a season.

Still, any time you have a coach who has established team-oriented goals and objectives and a group of parents, each of whom has the primary goal of making sure that his or her child has the best possible individual experience, there are going to be differences in opinion. This is true no matter how well you communicate before or during the season.

The majority of parents have a few major concerns, and if those concerns are addressed, you likely won't hear a negative word from them all season. Those parents want to know that their kids are safe, are getting an opportunity to participate, and are having a good time. If they can drop their children off at practice without a worry and can come watch their kids play and see that they are active, laughing and smiling, as far as they are concerned it's mission accomplished.

Dealing with parents can become a little more difficult if a particular parent thinks he or she is more of an "expert" than you about your sport, if the parent is more concerned about winning and losing than you are, or if the parent thinks that he or she is raising a budding superstar who should play every inning of every game. If this particular child isn't playing a primary position at all times, in the parent's view, the coach is hurting the team's chances of winning and limiting the child's athletic development.

In these cases, when it is obvious that the parents' and coach's goals are not aligned, there are going to be differences in opinion. The extent of these differences and their effect on the other team members, the coaches, and the other parents will be determined by how they are handled on both sides.

Setting Expectations and Sticking to Your Plan

When you coach at the youngest levels, external pressures to win are obviously far fewer, or completely nonexistent, compared to the high school level. These pressures tend to escalate a little bit every time you progress up the ladder to a new age group or a new level of play. There are travel baseball teams these days for kids as young as 7 or 8 years old. In some ways this is great, because it gives kids who really love the game and have progressed a little bit faster than the average recreational player an opportunity to play more games against other players of similar skill levels. In other ways this can be dangerous, because a lot of parents and coaches attach an automatic increase in intensity and pressure to win to a team that is playing travel ball.

These increases in intensity and pressure, as well as a more grueling practice and game schedule, can lead to an atmosphere that is more likely to cause a distaste for the game among the players and eventually lead to burnout. It also can lead to an environment in which parents expect the coaches to try to win at all costs and play only the best players the majority of the time. All over the country we are finding that parents who don't agree with the decisions made by the coaches of their children's teams—whether those decisions are about general philosophy, the composition of the team, or playing time—are going off on their own and starting their own teams. Although this has caused a phenomenal expansion in the number of travel teams and more opportunities for kids to play at higher levels, it does not set a good example for our children. By taking this approach, parents essentially are telling their kids that it's okay to do what is best for them if they don't get their way. Ideally, if we can educate coaches on the proper way to communicate with parents so that everyone is on the same page, we can make the overall experience better for players and parents at all levels and eliminate some of these disagreements and defections.

Even though the kids on the travel teams have shown an affinity and an aptitude for the game of baseball, these programs still are developmental, which means that the main objectives should be fundamental skill development, fun, and equal participation. No kid age 13 or younger should ever spend the majority of his or her time sitting on the bench. In fact, even as you progress to the freshman and junior varsity levels, we are still talking about developmental programs. A kid who is forced to sit and watch is going to look for another activity that is more fun.

Kids who sit on the bench most of the time aren't going to have much fun. It is important to keep all of your players engaged during games and practices.

Of course, at some point there will come a time at which kids will have to try out for a team and face the possibility of being cut. This is a fact of life, and when handled correctly by the head coach, getting cut from a team can teach a valuable lesson and help a young athlete grow as a person. However, if there are enough kids who don't make the first team and still love the game, we're doing the game and those kids a major disservice if we as coaches and parents don't try to provide them with an opportunity to continue playing the game on an organized team that will allow them to further develop their skills and love of the game. So many kids these days are late bloomers. It would be great for them and for baseball if we could make sure opportunities exist for these players to continue playing so that they don't give up on baseball and jump to other sports. We hope that by providing more educational materials for youth baseball coaches, we can keep kids playing baseball in a way that brings them the enjoyment and self-improvement they need to maintain interest.

As we have said several times already, the most important step coaches can take to prevent parental pressures about winning as well as questions about playing time is to communicate their philosophies up front. If any parents disagree at that point, most likely they will still have time to find another program for their child. If any parents disagree or have reservations and you stick to your plan throughout the season, they won't have any ground to stand on if they didn't communicate their concerns initially and a problem arises down the road.

Your preseason meeting will be rendered meaningless if you don't follow through on everything you discuss. However, as long as you stick to the plan, have well-thought-out reasons for everything you do, and keep the lines of communication open all season, you can rest easy, knowing that you've done all that you can and that the parents had their opportunity to question you or opt out of the program before practice started. Most important, if you do hold true to your professed philosophies and methods, the majority of parents will be pleased with your efforts.

Problems often arise when several parents have similar issues with a coach, and they band together in an attempt to undermine his or her authority. The momentum can build, and if these parents can make a case that you were not forthright from the beginning, they can even sway parents who were previously happy with you. If a large group of parents isn't supporting the coach and team members begin sensing this, the coach's authority and ability to control the team can be diminished quickly, creating an atmosphere of chaos and selfishness. Obviously, this is neither a healthy nor an enjoyable environment for anyone involved with the team.

By communicating your philosophies up front, following through on them, and keeping the lines of communication open throughout the season, it is very likely that you will meet little resistance from parents. There are exceptions to every rule, though, and if you do run into a disagreement, be willing to discuss the situation with the parent either via phone or in person—not through e-mail. Remind the parent of what you talked about in your preseason meeting, and show him or her how you have followed through on that plan. Show the parent that you told him or her up front what to expect and that there was every opportunity to question you or try another program at that point. Prepare examples of how you have stuck to your plan and how the team is progressing.

Many times a child may be having a great time playing on a certain team, but a parent still has a problem with the coach. Find out from the child if he or she is having a good time and why or why not. If the child is having fun, relay this conversation to the parent, reminding him or her about your goals for the team and that youth baseball is intended to be for the kids and not the parents. The reality is that no matter what you do as a coach, you are going to run into people who disagree with your methods and will be unhappy with you. If you have communicated your plan from the start, stayed on course throughout the season, are organized and prepared at all times, and have maintained an open line of communication, you have done all that you possibly can as a coach. Don't let one difficult parent ruin the experience for you, because if you have communicated properly, you will have many ardent supporters among your team's parents.

Handling the "Expert" Parent

Sometimes you will run across a well-meaning "expert" parent who has an endless supply of ideas about drills, plays, or lineup combinations. This parent might know a lot less about the game than he or she thinks, might simply be trying to have you implement something to benefit his or her child, or could be a potential assistant coach. Part of successful communication with parents is showing a willingness to politely listen and respond to their suggestions.

Of course, you don't have to implement every suggestion that you get from a parent. But don't shut yourself off to their ideas, either. You might run into an energetic parent with coaching experience and a love for the game who has some great suggestions. It is not a sign of weakness or lack of knowledge to try a drill or practice idea that is given to you by a parent. You might find that their idea really benefits your team and makes your practices better.

If you find an energetic parent with some good ideas, put this person at the head of your list of potential assistant coaches, letting him or her know that you would love some help on the field whenever possible, even if it's just occasionally. Let the parent know that you always welcome assistance and that whatever he or she could do for the team would make your life easier. If the parent can't actively assist, invite more ideas and implement the ones you think will benefit the team.

You will occasionally run into overzealous parents who really don't know the game or might be trying to be involved to the point that their child gets preferential treatment. Again, always be willing to listen to their ideas. Keep the line of communication open and be polite. Thank them for their willingness to help while letting them know that you have a good sense of the team's skill level and know the best ways to help the players improve. Tell them that you have run across hundreds of great ideas that you wish you could try but just haven't found the time to fit them into the practice routine. Thank them again for their support and encourage them to continue bringing you ideas. This will make them feel good, might actually lead to a good practice idea or two, and will show everyone that you are willing to communicate with parents at any time.

Keeping Your Distance

Something that you will run into at all levels of coaching is a parent (or two, or six!) who feels a need to be close to his or her child. Of course, at the very youngest age groups, there is going to be more active parental participation. For T-ballers, there might be some separation anxiety or fear—among parents and kids—that causes parents to want to be close to their children or the kids to ask for their parents to participate. It will get to the point sometimes at T-ball games where you see a parent standing with a player at every position.

While this is understandable, it can create problems. The level of parental participation, as well as the need and desire for parents to be close to their children, dissipates as the kids get older. However, you will still see parents who come and talk to their kids on the bench or stand close to the bench and yell instructions to the players on the field right up through high school. These situations can create an array of problems and distractions.

At the younger levels, you'll have to use your best judgment. Two or three coaches on the field to help with positioning and to give instructions should be sufficient. If there are many parents and coaches all shouting instructions, the kids can become confused. In fact, when the ball is hit to one of them and everyone is shouting something different, you can almost see a sense of panic on a player's face. Also, too many parents on the field can present obstacles for players attempting to field balls, and for some reason there always seems to be a parent who wants to stop a ball that is rolling in his or her direction. Try to allow only coaches on the field except in extreme instances when you feel that a player simply can't function without mom or dad nearby. If you're fortunate enough to be in a situation where many parents want to assist you, consider establishing a rotation in which two or three different people assist you each week.

As players progress it becomes imperative to maintain order on the bench. Parents other than coaches and assistants should never be in the area of the bench or dugout. If a parent wants to sit in a lawn chair down the third baseline and shout instructions to the team, there's not much you can do about that other than to ask that he or she leave the coaching to you and your staff. At least the kids are aware that instructions coming from that general direction are not coming from the coaches. Children, for the most part, seem to listen more to their coaches than their parents, anyway.

Real problems start to arise when parents invade the bench area. First, if they're sitting or standing close to the bench and shouting instructions, players might be confused about who's talking to them. This is especially problematic when parental advice contradicts what the coach believes. Second, the bench or dugout area is usually pretty small, so when you add a few adults to the mix, the space can get crowded and chaotic. Third, as a coach, you really don't want to turn around and see a parent sitting next to one of your players offering individual coaching advice that might differ from what you teach.

At your preseason meeting, make it clear that the bench or dugout area is off-limits to parents during games. If a player needs to talk to a parent or to get a drink, he or she should ask the coach if it is okay to run over to the parent between innings. This will be a quick visit, not a consultation. Make sure the parents understand that you want their support and that the kids need encouragement at all times, but stress that they should refrain from offering coaching advice during the game. Do this politely so they don't think you are suggesting that they don't know anything about the game. Point out the confusion that can set in when several adults are giving different instructions during a contest. Again, if you have a lot of parents who want to help, set up a rotation in which one of them (or more if you're short-handed) can help out at games and practices during a particular week.

The designated parents would serve as part of the coaching staff that week and would be permitted in the bench area. As in most life situations, showing a willingness to compromise and making an effort to accommodate people's needs can go a long way toward building positive relationships with parents.

Being Proactive

Addressing parents can be a difficult and sensitive issue for coaches. Failure to take control and set some ground rules before the season can be disastrous, however. Most times, if parents sense that the coach has a plan and understand that all he wants to do is to provide their children with the best possible experience, they will be much easier to deal with. There are always going to be parents who cross the line in one way or another. Some parents will continually cross the line. As a coach, if you set the parameters up front and explain why you approach things the way you do, your chances are pretty good of creating the atmosphere of teamwork, good sportsmanship, cooperation, and support that you desire, among players and parents. You might even want to consider giving parents something to sign off on indicating that they understand your philosophy and agree not to challenge your authority during the course of the season.

If you are not proactive, however, and you choose to avoid the parental issue altogether prior to the season, you will find it nearly impossible to successfully address the issues as they arise throughout the campaign. This can lead to public second guessing, criticism, and a lack of respect toward you from the parents. As we know, parental attitudes often filter down to their kids, which can create an atmosphere that is completely opposite of what you are hoping to establish.

Coaching Parents

The number one priority for youth baseball coaches should be to provide the best baseball experience possible for their players. One part of this process often overlooked is coaching the parents.

This doesn't mean that you should be trying to teach the parents to understand the game better or to have them master the game's skills. Instead, it means that as a coach you should help them understand their role in maximizing their child's overall baseball experience.

We have stressed the importance of holding a preseason meeting with parents to discuss your teaching philosophies, feelings about playing time, and the schedule of practices and games, and we have recommended enlisting parental support at practices or games. One other thing that you can communicate to parents is how they can become good baseball parents. This can be done via a handout or by simply speaking to them about their roles in creating a positive experience for everyone involved. Some ideas follow. You may want to consider using these concepts to form your own parental code of conduct.

Reinforce the Concept of Teamwork

How many times have you attended a youth baseball game and noticed a parent who cheers only for his or her child? This probably happens at one time or another during every youth sporting event played in this country. As a coach, it can be really hard to teach young players the importance of supporting their teammates or playing within a team concept if their parents cheer only for them. Explain to the parents that your job as a coach is to provide an all-around educational experience for the players. Tell them that one of the greatest life lessons that baseball teaches, one that carries over into almost every facet of our daily lives, is the importance of teamwork. Parents are the most influential figures in most kids' lives, so stress to them that you want them cheering for all of the players or none of the players. Likewise, make sure to tell parents that you would like them to make a point to congratulate every player after every game, win or lose.

Maintain an Even Keel

It's easy to cheer, scream, and be happy when your child's team scores 11 runs in the first inning. It's much harder to mask your disappointment when that same team falls behind 12 to 11 in the sixth. Kids feed off the atmosphere at the ballpark. If everyone is full of laughter, smiles, and support when things are going great and dead silent when adversity hits, don't you think the players are going to sense that and put more pressure on themselves?

Remember that winning is not the ultimate goal when it comes to youth baseball. Making sure that the kids have a good time and learn something are the most important goals. Coaches should tell parents to maintain an even keel—don't get too high or too low—and then lead by example. The last thing we want is for kids to be standing on the field feeling like failures. Also keep in mind that older travel team and high school players are still impressionable, maturing young people who feed off the signals they receive from adults. Maintaining an even keel among coaches and parents is just as important at these levels.

Another thing to be conscious of when it comes to maintaining an even keel is excessive criticism toward an individual player or the entire team. Remember that we are dealing with kids who are fragile. One negative experience can cause someone to give up the game forever. Mental or physical mistakes should never be addressed by coaches or parents in public view on the field. If a kid messes up, believe us, he or she knows it. Pointing it out in front of everyone, even in an instructive manner, is not going to help that player's mental state or make him or her a better player. Coaches should wait until the player comes off the field, and parents probably should wait until well after the game, either that night after they get home or even the next day. Nothing does more to shatter a young player's self-confidence or self-esteem than correcting or reprimanding the player publicly. Make it clear to parents that you are the coach and will handle everything that happens on the field during the next practice.

Don't Blame the Umpires

We all know that umpires make mistakes, but only in extremely rare instances does an umpire cost a team a game. One of our primary goals as youth baseball coaches should be to teach the kids the importance of respecting authority. Like the police in your hometown, umpires are the voice of authority on the baseball field and should be treated as such. Coaches must tell parents prior to the season that verbal abuse of umpires will not be tolerated, not because umpires are always right, but because of the message it sends to the players. Having respect for authority is one of our duties as American citizens. The coach is the only person who ever should be allowed to question an umpire, and when he does it always should be in a conversational, professional, and courteous manner.

Cheer for the Other Team

Parents can set a great example for their kids by cheering for the opposing team when there is an outstanding play or performance. Coaches can set the tone by shaking opposing players' hands, helping them up if they are injured, or telling them that they did something well. Most times, parents will pick up on this and join in. Soon, the players on the team will start following suit, and the team will get a reputation for good sportsmanship, win or lose. Like teamwork, winning and losing graciously is a lesson that carries over to other aspects of our everyday lives and can earn us a tremendous amount of respect from our peers.

Coaching Your Own Child

Many, if not most, coaches get involved in youth baseball because they want to make sure that their children have a positive experience. The local league might be short on coaches and be looking for volunteers, or perhaps a parent who has a busy work week sees coaching as a way to spend some quality time with his or her child.

Some of these parents have a lot of baseball experience, and others have very little. Some have coached before, and others have never set foot on a field. All of them want their children to have a great experience, and none of them wants to show favoritism. This seeming contradiction can lead to some difficult situations for these coaches.

For parents coaching their own children, the golden rule is to treat your child just like everyone else on the team, in good times and in bad. It doesn't matter if your kid is one of the best players or one of the lesser-skilled players. On the one hand, don't give your child preferential treatment when it comes to playing time or a spot in the batting order. On the other hand, don't weigh your child down with unfair burdens that aren't placed on the other players. For example, don't ask your kid to always carry the team equipment or to make sure the other players are doing all the drills correctly. And, finally, be very careful not to discipline your child in a way that separates him or her from the others. You want your child to look forward to being on the baseball field, not dread what punishment you might inflict if practice isn't going well.

Balancing this dynamic can be difficult. The natural instincts are to protect your child, whereas the fear is that other parents will think that you are playing favorites. If your policy is to not argue with umpires—as it should be—make sure you don't question an umpire if your child is on the short end of a close call. If you reverse the batting order each inning, make sure that your child has to adhere to that rule. If every player sits out two innings, your kid should, too. Make sure that any personal disagreements that arise are handled at home and not in front of the team, and that your child is not disciplined at practice because he or she did something wrong at home.

There is always time before and after practices and games to give your child extra attention and to help him or her improve. But when the team is together on the field, make sure that you do the best that you can to give everyone equal attention and treatment.

As players get older and things such as designating team captains and handing out team awards become more a part of coaching, continue to go out of your way to treat your child the same way you treat the other team members. If you think that your kid is captain material, instead of appointing captains, let the team vote and be willing to stick with those selections. You can do the same thing for team awards, or you can even let the parents vote on these. By handling difficult situations in this manner, no one can question you, no matter what happens. The parents and team members can't accuse you of favorable treatment if your child is chosen, and your son or daughter can't accuse you of going out of your way not to acknowledge him or her. In the long run, recognition from teammates will mean more to your child than recognition from you.

Another thing to be wary of is singling out your child for mistakes made by the team or for overall lackluster play. Everyone is responsible in these situations. If you feel like you need to be a little more stern than usual to get through to your team, pull them aside away from everyone and address the situation. Don't let your need to have an outlet to release your pent-up frustration cause you to unfairly discipline your child.

Remember, when it comes to having your son or daughter on your team—no matter what level you are coaching—live by the golden rule: Treat your child the same way as every other team member. If you can manage to do that, your life will be easier on and off the field.

Understanding Limits

Youth baseball seasons seem to be starting earlier each year. For many kids as young as 8 and 9 years old, baseball has become a year-round sport. In some ways it is exciting to see so many young people taking the sport seriously. As parents, however, we have unanswered questions about whether the game is becoming too serious too fast.

Just like most parents, we've wrestled with the question of how much is too much. On the developmental side, there is sentiment that the more a kid plays, the better he or she will get. This might be true in terms of preparation, but when it comes to kids, other factors will determine how well they play the game. First, some kids mature faster than others. They become bigger and stronger and are dominant players at a certain age no matter how much they play. Often, these players come back to the pack as they get older and other players catch up to them physically.

We have run into parents who hope to develop their children into the next Alex Rodriguez by literally standing over them and forcing them to play and practice baseball as much as possible. One parent we spoke to equated practicing baseball to homework: "If my son is going to spend two hours on homework, he's going to spend two hours playing baseball," the parent said. "Well, how does he like it?" we asked. The parent responded, "He doesn't like it at all, but someday he'll thank me."

This is the mentality that worries us most, but there's an argument to be made that if a kid does enjoy being on the field and wants to play every day, we as parents should try to accommodate those wishes. Some travel teams can play 65 or 70 games in a season. It's hard for us to recall playing in that many games as children, but what we do recall vividly is having a glove on our hands almost every day during the summer. Back then we played pick-up games, played games with plastic bats and balls, and even invented fun baseball games.

There weren't many summer days when we weren't playing baseball in some shape or form. Today, maybe all of those extra organized games make up for the fact that kids don't play pick-up or sandlot baseball anymore. But we are still concerned about the amount of pressure that can develop during organized games as opposed to the neighborhood sandlot games we used to play. We've been observing our kids and others who come to our academy the past few summers to monitor their level of enjoyment as well as their energy level. As coaches, it's really all about staying in tune with the players' needs and desires. We have kept a close watch in an attempt to find the proper balance and notice any warning signs that could indicate burnout.

At the developmental stages it is important for us to grow and nurture the seed. If a kid is playing baseball, he or she obviously is interested in and excited by the sport. Games can be fun, but they also can be pressure-packed, especially in a tournament environment. We have to be extremely careful not to zap the passion and fun from the game for the kids. Baseball is a sport with a lot of ups and downs. It is emotionally and mentally challenging. There is a danger, especially when things are not going so well, that baseball can become too much like work when there are so many games. This can lead to burnout and cause players to stop playing the sport, which is the exact opposite of what youth coaches should be trying to accomplish.

Another thing that worries us about kids playing so many games is the proper development of fundamental skills. When there are so many games, there isn't much time to practice. When placed in so many different game situations, kids naturally adapt to the size of the field as well as the speed of the game. Through trial and error they quickly figure out how to be successful at the level in which they

Teaching the fundamentals is important, but be careful not to get too serious too fast. Have fun at practice and your players will have fun, too.

are playing. For example, an infielder playing on a 60-foot diamond might be able to avoid backhanding balls and still throw runners out at first, because the players at his or her level are not that fast yet.

As the player grows older and plays on a bigger field, that same infielder might try to get in front of a ball to his or her right and then have to take a few extra steps to stop his or her momentum, set up, and make a strong throw. The extra time needed to make the play and the distance of the throw might allow a faster runner to reach base safely. If the player had learned how to properly backhand a ball earlier in his or her baseball career, he or she might have been able to make the play correctly and throw the runner out at first. The backhand is a skill that should be taught and practiced at the youngest ages. It is hard to develop a fundamental skill without practicing it over and over. Game situations do not provide enough opportunities to develop the muscle memory necessary to perfect certain fundamentals.

Remember that even though these kids are playing in a lot of games, they're still in the developmental stages. Practice is an essential tool for developing fundamentals. Kids get all wound up when they are getting ready to play games. While the games are being played, they are nervous and excited. There is pressure to succeed that doesn't exist in practice. Sure, you can work on certain things during batting practice and pregame infield, but the time for pregame practice is limited. Many times another game is going on and a team's pregame preparation takes place in an open field somewhere, not even on a baseball field.

Teaching fundamentals, both from a team and an individual standpoint, also is difficult during games. When a player makes a mistake you don't want to correct him or her on the field in front of everyone. That can be embarrassing and makes for a very negative experience. The best time to talk to a player about something that occurred during the game is between innings, but even then it is hard to communicate effectively. Coaches have other responsibilities they must tend to, such as coaching the bases. Parents are cheering, making noise, and trying to talk to their children. The player is worried about his next at-bat, whether his girlfriend saw him make a mistake, or what his parents are thinking. The excitement and pressure surrounding an organized game is simply not an environment conducive to teaching successfully.

So, practice is extremely important for developing the fundamental skills necessary for players to be successful as they continue climbing the youth baseball ladder. Practice also is essential for teaching team fundamentals and allowing players to learn about the nuances of the game. Baseball is the most cerebral team sport. Team strategies and individual responsibilities can change with each pitch. There is no way that all of these team fundamentals and strategies can be communicated and corrected within a hectic game environment.

Of course, there are positives that can come out of playing so many games during a season. To succeed in most tournaments, especially when they come in the middle of the regular-season schedule, teams need to develop pitching depth. This means that more kids will get the opportunity to pitch. The same can hold true for other positions. When you are playing so many games you have to make sure to spread the innings around or players will get tired, and their production—and ultimately their enjoyment of the sport—will tail off.

Ultimately, the coach of any team playing an extensive schedule is going to have to shoulder the responsibility of making the experience

Teach Proper Fundamental Approaches at Every Level

Cal Ripken, Jr.

Playing a variety of sports rather than specializing in baseball provides both mental and physical benefits to players of all ages. Too much of one sport can lead to physical burnout in the form of overuse injuries as well as mental burnout when the game becomes too much like work and ceases to be fun.

There is another area of concern when it comes to specializing in one sport. Every time an athlete steps up to a higher level—whether it's going from a recreational team to a travel team or from 60- or 70-foot bases to a regulation-sized diamond—he or she must leave behind some skills and replace them with new ones in order to compete successfully.

Kids who play baseball year-round might play in 70 or more games during a calendar year. When young athletes play one sport that much they naturally learn what it takes to be successful at their particular level of play. Because of this, they may develop shortcuts or methods that will not be effective when they move up to the next level, and these habits may become so ingrained that they are hard to break.

Let's look at the backhand as an example. Young players who compete on smaller fields can eliminate the backhand by learning how to round and charge a ground ball. They perfect this skill, and it can help them succeed on the smaller diamonds. However, because they have done this so often and had success with it, when they move up to a bigger field they often are unwilling or unable to let go of that skill and learn the backhand. It is imperative for players to use the backhand on regulation-sized fields for balls that are hit in the hole between third and short, because doing so allows them to get rid of the ball more quickly, which can be the difference between an out and a hit when such a long throw is required.

Another example is hitting. A pitcher who throws 80 miles per hour from 46 or 50 feet can get the pitch to home plate even more quickly than the hardest-throwing big league pitchers can. Young hitters learn to cheat and stride before the ball is even released. They shift their weight forward early and learn how to hit with a short, flick swing. Hitters who do this over and over really struggle when they move to the bigger diamond. They tend to shift their weight too

(continued)

(continued)

soon and are susceptible to off-speed and breaking pitches. Good hitters are able to let the ball travel before deciding how to attack the pitch. Players who have played hundreds of games as front-foot hitters really struggle making that adjustment.

It is our hope that this book will help you teach your players to approach the game so that it will bring them success and enjoyment into their teen years and beyond. The bottom line is to let the kids determine how much baseball they play and to encourage them to try other sports in hopes of developing all-around athleticism and avoiding physical and mental burnout.

as positive as possible. How the season is framed or presented to the kids is incredibly important. The coach must be in tune to the needs and desires of the kids to make sure they're not burning out. He or she must determine if they are still having fun and looking forward to games. He or she must do everything possible to make the game experiences enjoyable and to foster an environment in which everyone contributes. He or she must avoid the win-at-all-costs mentality and not rely on the same players over and over again. He or she must maintain an even keel, not getting too high or too low. And most important, the coach must monitor the situation closely at all times, watching for signs of physical and mental fatigue. In theory, playing more games can be a good thing if the situation is handled correctly, but a lot rides on the coach.

Playing Other Sports

Most people think that our dad, Cal Ripken, Sr., pushed us to become big league players by making us play baseball and drilling us on the finer points of the game nonstop. Actually, nothing could be further from the truth. Dad allowed us to discover the game and develop our feelings about it on our own.

Of course, we had plenty of opportunities to develop a love for the game of baseball. We had the luxury of being around professional ballparks and professional players for most of our childhoods, which created a certain excitement surrounding the game for us. We watched our father closely and noticed the joy he felt every time he put on his uniform and took the field. If it was that much fun for him, then why wouldn't we want to play, right? But it was always our decision. Dad never pushed us at all.

As a matter of fact, Dad actually encouraged us to put our gloves away at the end of the summer. He was a very good soccer player and seemed to enjoy teaching and playing that sport, too. In addition to soccer, we both developed a love for the game of basketball and played that in the off-season as well. Later, as our baseball careers developed, we found that basketball was a great way to stay in shape during the off-season.

Probably because of Dad, as well as our love for sports in general, we feel pretty strongly about allowing kids to play other sports in the off-season. We do not favor specialization. Kids who play different sports throughout the year are more likely to avoid burnout and will develop their overall athleticism. If their athleticism improves, it stands to reason they will improve as baseball players. Playing soccer allows kids to develop better balance and agility because it really is the one sport in which you use only your feet. Basketball movements are more explosive, helping improve power, quickness, and lateral mobility. Playing other sports allows the main muscle groups used in baseball to rest while providing an opportunity for other muscles and athletic skills to be developed.

Taking some time off from baseball also seems to allow the flame to rekindle during the off-season, generating a feeling of excitement toward the game as the spring approaches. This is not to say that a kid should never pick up a ball during the fall and winter months. If a kid enjoys playing catch or going to the local batting cage to hit, by all means let it happen. Just let the kid dictate. Don't force it. Throwing and hitting a little bit during the winter months can help keep the body's muscles in baseball condition and keep players' reflexes sharp. Those are good things, but only if the kid is allowed to make the decision about when and how much to practice.

The key from a coaching standpoint is to keep the kids' best interests in mind when it comes to any athletic activity. Kids are driven by fun. If they're not having fun, you'll know it. They will be reluctant to go to practice and will perform sluggishly when they are there. Monitor your team's progress and keep these warning signs in mind. If players ask to take a day off or to try another sport, let them give it a shot. Maybe they will miss baseball and be more excited to come back and play it again. Or perhaps they will fall in love with another activity and get years of enjoyment from it. Either way, the kids win, and that's what's most important.

3

Reasonable Expectations

Youth baseball coaches often fall into the trap of trying to teach too much. Remember that baseball is a simple game. In general, the teams that throw, catch, and hit the best are the teams with the most success. What determines whether a game, practice, or season is successful? The answer to that depends on the age group and the level of play. Success in youth baseball should never be determined by the number of wins and losses. In fact, winning should be way down on the list of priorities. If the baseball experience is enjoyable for the kids and they learn something, we should feel very good about that as coaches.

Even as players get older and competition intensifies, right up through the high school level, it's important to understand that we're dealing with kids and that kids are fragile. One negative experience can tarnish a player's view of the sport for life. Neither an error nor a single lost game is worth turning a player off to baseball. At the youngest levels, most players we coach won't play for their high school teams. At the high school level, most players won't play in college. Even at the college level, a very small fraction of players will go on to play professionally.

As coaches, our responsibility to the game of baseball is to create a positive, organized, enjoyable environment that promotes a love of the game within the players. If one of our players has a bad experience and stops playing baseball, the chances are good that none of his or her children will play the game, either. And maybe none of his or her children's children will play. The effect of that one bad experience multiplies, especially with so many recreational activities vying for our young people's attention. And you can bet that if one player is turned off to the game by a coach, others will follow. Most kids are followers, not leaders. The effect of that negative situation can be devastating to the game's health if repeated consistently around the country.

Coaches must set goals for their teams and celebrate all successes, small and large. There are general goals that cut across all age levels and there are age-specific goals. If these goals are accomplished, regardless of the team's ultimate win–loss record, the season should be considered a success. Sometimes all goals are not attained. Circumstances beyond our control can intervene to prevent us from accomplishing some things we set out to accomplish. In such cases, it's human nature for coaches to be hard on themselves. Instead of beating yourself up too much, look back at what you might have been able to change to accomplish more. And remember: If the kids had fun and learned something, the experience was more than worthwhile. At Ripken Baseball, one of our core philosophies is, "Look to the future and learn from the past." There is always room for improvement. Even teams that win the World Series can improve. Just look at the off-season roster moves that championship teams make every year. If you use the general and age-specific goals we present in this book as guidelines, and you do everything in your power to help your team accomplish those goals within the context of an environment that stresses fun and learning, everything will turn out fine.

Goals for All Ages

There are basic goals that all baseball coaches—even coaches at the highest levels—should strive to accomplish with their teams. In the broadest sense these goals are a good barometer of how successful the season was from a coaching perspective. As a coach, continually ask yourselves these questions to help determine if you're on the right track.

Are the Kids Having Fun?

Baseball is a game. We stress that over and over in this book. It should be fun. You can tell very easily if a group of kids is having fun. Do

Even for a young player, success increases confidence and feeds the desire to learn more.

they move quickly to the field when they arrive, or do they have to be forced to play? Are they smiling when they're on the field, or do they appear to be sad or bored? Is there a lot of laughter and energy, or are the kids lethargic? Do they ask to stay and practice or play longer, or do they want to leave early?

Kids are not hard to read. If they're having fun, keep doing what you're doing. If they appear lethargic, sluggish, bored, or unhappy, take a look at what you're doing and make some adjustments. Remember that kids of all ages have limited attention spans. Keep them in small groups. Keep them active and moving around. Provide them with a variety of activities. Turn drills into contests. Give out prizes. Give your players nicknames. Create a rotation in which every player gets to play each position. (At the youngest levels this is important so that players can develop all the fundamental skills they need to play baseball. As kids get older, it's to their benefit to be able to play several positions if they hope to continue playing at higher levels.) Yell and scream in a positive manner. Act goofy. Have a sense of humor. Enjoy yourself. If the coach is having fun, chances are the team is having fun. If the team is having fun, there's a good chance players will come back for more the following year. That's the ultimate goal.

Are the Kids Improving?

One of the most rewarding things about coaching youth baseball is getting to see players improve. It's not a stretch to say that kids can improve each and every time they practice. At our camps we often have groups of kids who have trouble playing catch at the beginning of the week. By the end of the week we see some of these same kids turning double plays in our daily camp games.

The next section of this chapter deals with age-specific goals. There we get into a deeper discussion of motor skill development and which types of skills can be taught successfully at different ages. It's important that the skills that are emphasized are not too difficult for the kids to master. Kids have an innate desire to learn and improve. When they're successful, and those successes are celebrated, the thirst to learn more increases. Coaches have a responsibility to put players in position to experience success and then go out of their way to point out the improvement. This sounds like an oversimplification, but just like throwing and catching, success and positive reinforcement are as important for the 8-year-old as they are for the 22-year-old.

Are the Kids Learning?

Every day at our camps we make a point to review what we did the day before. At the beginning of each session we ask questions about what was covered the previous day to reinforce the lessons and make sure the concepts were understood and absorbed. If we find that kids are struggling with a lesson or concept, we spend more time on the review to make sure they have grasped the lesson completely. If the kids understand everything, we move on to a new lesson. The following day we repeat the process, reviewing everything that we've taught to that point.

It is important for coaches to make sure that their players are learning something in addition to having fun. Learning and fun go hand in hand. As kids learn and understand, they get better and want to learn more. When they improve, they have more fun. By keeping kids active and being creative you can make sure that they learn while having fun. If kids are having fun, they often don't realize that they're learning or practicing, which means you can hold their attention longer. This leads to more efficient and effective practices.

When coaching, especially when dealing with skills that build upon one another, it's important to review and make sure players have grasped the initial lesson before you introduce something more complex. Introducing new concepts that players aren't prepared for

Playing Up: Don't Rush It!

Cal Ripken, Jr.

I often get asked whether I believe in letting younger players play up. By "playing up" I mean allowing kids to play in an age group older than where they're supposed to play. There really is no one answer to suit everybody. Kids develop mentally and physically at different rates, so each case must be looked at on an individual basis.

If kids possess the skill sets and are mentally capable of playing with older players, in most cases I would not have a problem with playing them up. For the past several years, my son Ryan has played up on his teams, which means he's usually the youngest on his team. Ryan has always been pretty big for his age, and his skill level fit in well with the kids he was playing with, so the experience has been good for him.

As an 11-year-old, Ryan played on a 12-year-old travel team. In previous years he had played on similar teams, but I had limited the number of games that he could participate in to keep him from burning out. With his team slated to play more than 70 games last year, I was a little concerned about how he would handle it, but he made it through, enjoyed the experience, and had some success.

Still, as Ryan approached the age at which the field was going to start to get bigger, I thought it would be a good idea to let him play with kids his own age to give his body and skills a catch-up year.

Doing this allows a young player to be more successful or dominant, which tends to help his or her confidence. It also can allow a kid to assume different roles within the framework of a team, going from being just another player to being a key performer and possibly from being a follower to a leader.

Like Ryan, I spent most of my formative years playing up on various baseball teams. When I was 16, however, I had an opportunity to stay back and play with kids my own age. That experience was very positive for me and is one I would recommend for players who always feel the pressure to be at their best in order to play with an older age group.

Don't be afraid to allow a player who is physically and mentally capable to play up if the situation arises. Also don't be afraid of hurting a player's or parent's feelings by suggesting that the player take a year to play with kids his or her own age. Just remember that

(continued)

(continued)

kids who play up always feel that they have to be at their best to compete. Giving them a break and allowing them to play with kids their own age on occasion gives them an opportunity to relax and build their confidence.

As we said in the first chapter, baseball gets serious fast enough. As coaches, we need to look at what's good for each individual, not just for the team. No matter what decision you make, if you frame it properly, you can usually ease parents' concerns and help them see that you're looking out for their child's best interests.

can lead to failure. Repeated failure often leads to frustration. Frustration can cause kids to quit playing baseball.

At our camps we like to use buzzwords to emphasize our teaching points. For example, for the soft toss hitting drill, we want kids to concentrate on "loose hands, quick bat." For weight shift and hitting off of a tee, we say, "Go back to go forward." In the infield we catch a ground ball with a "wide base, butt down, hands out in front." You'll catch us using these buzzwords throughout the book. Use them yourself to help your players absorb the lessons you teach them. Try to come up with some terms of your own. Do whatever it takes to help your players learn what you're trying to teach them.

Age-Specific Goals

For the purposes of teaching baseball effectively, we have divided all players into the following age groups: 4 to 6, 7 to 9, 10 to 12, 13 to 14, and 15 and up. Some kids mature physically much faster than others. Motor skill development varies as well, but for the most part you can teach similar skills to the kids within these separate age breakdowns and have them experience success. If you look at the breakdowns, the 4-to-6 age group represents the beginners who usually play T-ball. At ages 7 to 9, fine motor skill development has progressed to the point that most kids possess the ability to learn to catch and hit a pitched ball. The 10-to-12 age group is when players begin to decide for themselves that they like baseball and might want to pursue it a little more seriously. We separated the 13-to-14 age group because these players are trying to make the adjustment to the 80- or

90-foot diamond while waiting for their bodies to mature physically. Once players turn 15 they are generally fairly serious and capable of executing most, if not all, of the skills and strategies necessary to play baseball at a high level.

We believe strongly in keeping things simple when teaching the game of baseball. With that in mind, we have developed five goal areas for each of these age groups. You'll want to keep these five goal areas in mind every time you plan a practice. They represent the fundamental building blocks for success. The goals at one level need to be accomplished before the goals at the next level can be pursued. If this happens, great! Consider yourself an expert coach. But, don't feel that you've failed if you don't get beyond the goals for a particular age group. If your team achieves these basic goals, you should consider your season a success. If you don't reach the goals, that's okay, too. Stress all of the positive things that were accomplished and try to figure out how to accomplish all of your goals the next season. Remember: Look to the future and learn from the past.

If you're coaching a team of 7-year-olds and it's obvious that they have not mastered the concepts and skills set forth in the age-appropriate goals for the 4-to-6 age group, it's imperative that you go back and work with the players until they have achieved those goals before moving on to more advanced skills. On the other hand, if your team achieves the age-specific goals quickly, it might be worthwhile to jump ahead and attempt to accomplish some of the goals outlined for the next age group.

Always keep in mind that just as some kids mature faster than others, some kids will master fundamental skills faster than others. Stay in tune with each child's needs and abilities so that you can tailor your work with each player during a particular drill to suit his or her situation. For example, if you're working on catching ground balls properly, some kids will be ready to field balls that are rolled or hit harder or to one side or the other before others. You can either group kids according to skill level, or if that's impossible, make sure that you adapt the drill to meet everyone's individual needs and abilities on a player-by-player basis.

Five goals for the 4-to-6 age group

1. Learning the basic rules—the right direction to run when the ball is hit; runners must touch the bases; how to record outs (catch the ball in the air, throw to first, or tag the runners); running past first base; scoring a run; three outs constitute an inning.
2. Throwing mechanics—turn the body so that the front shoulder points toward the target; keep the elbow above the shoulder;

step toward the target with the nonthrowing foot and release the ball.

3. Tracking—follow the ball with the eyes into the glove, whether on the ground or in the air (use softer balls); use two hands to catch and field; try to catch the ball out in front of the body.

4. Hitting—how to hold and swing the bat; batting safety (when not to swing bats, wearing batting helmets); hitting off a tee; hitting softly tossed pitches.

5. Learning positional play—if the ball is hit to your buddy, let him or her field it (note to coach: try not to put more than 10 players on a field at a time).

Five goals for the 7-to-9 age group

1. Learning the basic rules—force outs; tagging up; baserunning (when you don't have to run; not running into or past team-mates on the basepaths); balls and strikes.

2. Throwing mechanics—introduce the four-seam grip; point the front shoulder, step, and throw; introduce the concept of gener-ating momentum toward the target and following the throw.

3. Catching and fielding—thrown and hit balls; fingers up versus fingers down; see the glove and the ball; use two hands; fore-hands and backhands; introduce the underhand flip; first-base fundamentals; crossover and drop steps.

4. Hitting—choosing the right bat; proper grip; hitting pitched balls; introduce drill work (tee, soft toss, short toss).

5. Learning positional play—learn the positions and the areas each player should cover; cover the nearest base when the ball is not hit to you; basics of cutoffs and relays.

Five goals for the 10-to-12 age group

1. Learning the basic rules—infield fly rule; balks.

2. Baserunning—leads; steals; extra-base hits.

3. Pitching and throwing mechanics—wind-up versus stretch; four-seam grip; shuffle, throw, follow; pitcher covering first.

4. Hitting—repetitions; drill work (tee, soft toss, short toss, stick-ball, lob toss, one-arm drill); bunting.

5. Learning team fundamentals—cutoffs and relays; basic bunt defenses; basic first-and-third situations; underhand flip (box drill) and double plays; defending the steal; infield and outfield communication and priorities.

Five goals for the 13-to-14 age group

1. Throwing mechanics and pitching—emphasis on generating momentum toward the target and following the throw (larger field); breaking balls; change-ups; pitching mechanics and using the body effectively (longer distance); pickoff mechanics; flatwork (drills); introduction to long toss.

2. Hitting—introduce situational hitting (inside-out swing; hitting behind runners; hit and run; productive outs); sacrifice bunting versus bunting for a hit; understanding the count.

3. Baserunning—first-and-third situations; steal breaks; delayed steals; reading situations and reacting to them.

4. Fielding—generating momentum back toward the target on throws when necessary; crossover and drop steps; backhands and when to use them; double-play depth; pitcher covering first; infield communication.

5. Learning team fundamentals—pickoff plays; full bunt defenses; full first-and-third defenses; pop-up and fly ball priorities; double plays and underhand flips.

Five goals for the 15+ age group

1. Throwing mechanics and pitching—long toss; flatwork (drills); continue mastering breaking and off-speed pitches; throwing for accuracy; generating momentum toward the target and following the throw; pickoff mechanics.

2. Hitting—mental aspects (hitter's count versus pitcher's count); two-strike hitting; aggressive versus defensive swings; situational hitting; productive outs; advanced game situations and defenses.

3. Baserunning—one-way leads; going on the first move; reacting to batted balls; tag-up situations; third-base rules; no-out, one-out, and two-out rules.

4. Fielding—understanding and adapting to playing conditions (grass versus dirt, sun, bad fields); fence drill (outfield); crossover and drop steps; do-or-die plays at the plate; preventing runners from taking extra bases; communicating between pitches.

5. Learning team fundamentals—cutoffs and relays (introduce the trailer concept); advanced pickoff plays (daylight play; plays put on by fielders) and when to use them; double plays; advanced game situations and defenses.

In later chapters we'll show you drill and practice plans to help you achieve the goals appropriate for the age level you're coaching. It's our goal to provide you with a basic practice framework and many different options to help you keep practices fresh and effective. Remember that this book is primarily designed to provide you with a solid plan to become an effective coach. Other Ripken instructional products go into more detail about skill development, drills, and team fundamentals. Future products will delve even deeper into the concepts of team fundamentals and strategies. This book, combined with our other resources, should arm you with everything you need to experience success as a baseball coach.

4

Baseball Practice Basics

When it comes to playing baseball, games are fun. No matter our age, we enjoy testing our skills against others. Even the youngest baseball players want to see how they compare to other players or teams their age. As parents, how many times have you tried to make your children move a little faster toward their destination by saying, "Hey, let's race. I bet you can't beat me!" Of course, even 2-, 3- and 4-year-olds want to compete and win. Learning to compete to the best of our ability at whatever we pursue and learning to win and lose with grace and dignity are important life lessons that should be introduced to children at a young age. But to maximize a young player's enjoyment of the game and to provide players with the best opportunity to improve, organized and enjoyable practices are a must.

The Importance of Practice

Make it fun. This is one of our basic philosophies when it comes to teaching baseball. Part of this means letting the kids play games, which we do every day at most of our camps. But when it comes to developing young baseball players—from T-ball right up through high school—the importance of practice, even during the season, cannot be underestimated.

Because kids enjoy games more than anything, it is important to provide plenty of game time for our young players. Games give the kids something to look forward to each week, which helps maintain their interest. How many games a team should play during a given week and over a season really depends on the age, interest level, and skill level of the players. Try not to overdo it at the youngest ages. Although baseball games lend themselves to down time—between pitches, between innings, during your team's turn at bat—games don't usually offer an atmosphere conducive to teaching. There's a lot of excitement and energy (and sometimes tension) surrounding games, as well as outside interference and distractions, all of which can make it extremely difficult to communicate any type of teaching to a player.

During games at our camps we make a point not to stop play to bring attention to a mistake or situation that could have been handled differently. We don't want to single out a kid to tell him or her that something could have been done different or better. That can lead to embarrassment, which might turn a young player off to baseball for good. We prefer to teach between innings in the quiet of the dugout or bench area. Still, at that time, players are most likely focusing on something else instead of giving you full attention. They might be looking at their parents, thinking about their next at-bat, or scanning the crowd in the stands for a friend.

For some of our camps we have developed a list of the most common mistakes or areas needing improvement. These issues are addressed in a special instructional session for all players attending the camp or through additional team instructional sessions before the next afternoon's games. This method avoids embarrassing any one player and provides an atmosphere that is conducive to communicating and learning. In our view, parents should even refrain from talking to their children about situations that occurred in games during the car ride home. At that point kids have had their fill of baseball for the day and are probably thinking about how hungry they are or which video game they want to play when they get to the house.

Instead of singling out a player or situation and trying to correct it right after it happens on the field in full view of everyone, wait until the inning is over and pull the players involved aside to discuss what happened and how it can be corrected the next time. Remember that there are a lot of distractions during games, so maintaining your team's attention can be challenging. When teaching a lesson or correcting a mistake, find a spot that's somewhat removed from parents and other spectators. Otherwise, the excitement will take away from the kids' ability to absorb the information.

Although it can be helpful to go over these situations after they happen, remember that the best time to teach is during practice. Kids seem to have the ability to let go of the moment and not dwell on what has just taken place. They are pretty good about looking ahead to their next activity. If you rehash every detail of the game during the contest or as soon as it's over, you run the risk of overloading your players with information and zapping the enjoyment from the game experience. Maintain a journal or notebook with a detailed list of situations and mistakes that need to be examined at the next practice. Keep the list to yourself until practice time and then run through everything that you want to address when you have everyone's full attention. Try your best to re-create the situations and present them as areas that the team needs to improve on rather than pointing out the mistakes made by one or two individuals.

Clearly, as we have stated, the best time to address situations that occur in games and to perfect areas of play that need work is during practice time. Leagues that only play games can really hurt the development of their young players. I would even argue that the more advanced travel teams, which play 50 or 60 games (or more) during the spring and summer (and sometimes into the fall and winter), might be hurting their players' development at times because they play too many games and don't allow enough time to address skill development and team fundamentals in a practice setting. Big league players go through six weeks of spring training for a reason. The players must get their repetitions, refine their fundamental skills, and develop their team strategies and philosophies over an extended period of time, because once the season begins they play almost every day. Having six weeks of practice before starting a season is hardly practical when it comes to kids, however. Issues such as field availability, inclement weather, and team members' involvement in other sports combine to limit the amount of preseason practice time a team gets.

Right up through high school, into college, and even at the professional level, the process of learning on the baseball field is a continual one. There's no way you can possibly simulate everything that potentially can happen during the course of a game in practices. Baseball is a crazy game. Every year, a bunch of plays occur over the course of a Major League season that we have never seen before. Big league players are the best in the world at what they do, and because they play so many games, they often have to learn on the fly. At the lower levels of baseball, we have the luxury of re-creating any new or unusual situations that arise in a practice setting to make sure that all of the tangible lessons can be absorbed. Adults are much more experienced at facing a situation or circumstance and adapting a response for the next time that situation arises without having to re-create the original scenario. For kids, having the opportunity to break the situation down into understandable parts and to explain why each player involved in the play should react in a certain way is an invaluable learning opportunity. If you do nothing but play games, it becomes difficult to do any teaching because you're always reacting to events that occur in the heat of battle.

Practice gets a bad rap, especially in baseball, for being boring and tedious. There are so many fine motor skills that must be mastered to play the sport—throwing, catching, hitting—that fundamental skill development is a must. Remember that in a sense, despite the complex strategies used by big league managers, baseball is essentially a simple game. Both young Ryan Ripken and Alex Rodriguez must be able to throw the ball, catch the ball, and hit the ball to be successful. Moreover, both Ryan and Alex should follow the exact same fundamental approaches to be successful. When a ground ball is hit to Ryan, if he has been schooled correctly, he will field it with his feet spread apart to create a wide base, his butt down, and his hands out in front. The same goes for Alex. Once Alex fields the ground ball, he should shuffle his feet toward the first baseman, step directly toward that target, and then follow the throw in that same direction. Ryan should do it the same way. When we instruct young players, we have them work on these simple fundamentals over and over. Why? Because those are the same fundamentals that Alex has worked on from the time he was playing recreational ball right up to this very day. Baseball's fundamental skills are very simple; the complexities of the game come with the various strategies and team fundamentals that are incorporated as we get older and the game becomes more serious. But those complexities can't be introduced until the basics are mastered.

Games provide kids with a fun, competitive atmosphere that's necessary to maintain their interest and attention. However, kids simply don't get enough repetitions in games to develop the fundamental skills they need to improve. There are many fun ways to introduce and work on the basic individual and team fundamentals during practice. We'll cover these throughout the book.

Run a Fun, Efficient Practice

We've all seen it. You walk by a local baseball field where a team's practice is going on. Young kids are scattered around the field looking lackadaisical and bored. An adult is pitching, one player is batting, another player is on deck, and the rest of the team is in the infield and outfield. It's hot, and the only person who looks interested is the batter. Even the coach looks as if he'd rather be elsewhere. A ball is hit, and one of the fielders half-heartedly chases the ball and throws it back into the infield. Balls are scattered everywhere. Now and then a player sits down or wanders into the bench area to get a drink. This goes on for an hour or so, and then everyone goes home. That's practice.

Unfortunately, this scenario plays out more often than not on baseball fields across America. It's easy to see why over the last 10 to 15 years many kids have become bored with baseball and look toward sports they find more exciting. The rise of extreme sports, such as skateboarding and trick cycling, has given kids more opportunities to pursue recreational activities on their own.

Home video games give kids the feeling that they are really playing sports in professional stadiums and arenas. It's easy to get a small group of friends together, find a basketball, and get a pick-up game started. Soccer and hockey have developed programs to train and certify coaches, and parents seem to prefer the idea of sending their kids into an environment that they know will be organized and structured.

The described batting practice scenario is not the only reason that baseball has struggled to hold onto its participants. In actuality, that scenario is more common as kids get a little older and their parents become less interested in volunteering. At the youngest ages, ages 4 to 6, when most kids play T-ball, parents are more eager to get out on the field and help ensure their kids are having a good time. Everyone wants video footage of their 5-year-old's first T-ball game. As the years pass, it brings us great joy to look back on our children's formative years with fondness. We love to rerun old videos of our kids having fun—even if they don't always appreciate it!

One of the big problems with baseball right now is that the game, as currently structured, is not a lot of fun for even the youngest players. We would argue that there are just as many (if not more) 4- and 5-year-olds who are as intrigued now as there have ever been when they see a baseball and a bat. They still want to throw or hit the ball. This is part of their natural curiosity. Kids want to learn to play baseball. So, what happens between the time of that first spark of interest and the age of 13, when kids seem to be dropping baseball for other recreational activities? We would argue that the baseball experience is not enjoyable for most kids from the earliest stages of their athletic development. It is our own opinion that this situation can be fixed.

We don't blame the volunteer coaches for the decline in baseball participation, or for the lack of excitement that kids seem to find in

Practice is the best time for the coach to teach players the fundamentals.

the game. Baseball as a sport has not given much attention to the needs of its coaches. Most times, coaches are not armed with the materials and knowledge they need about the game itself, motor development, and child psychology. They volunteer their time by checking a box on their child's registration form and are called and told when and where to pick up the equipment, team jerseys, and so on. From that point, it's up to them. Sometimes one designated practice time and one game time per week is assigned to each team. In other cases, there might be two games per week and no practices. At the youngest ages, the games often evolve into free-for-alls in which most of the defensive players jump on the batted ball while baserunners advance one base at a time. Very little learning occurs other than the players gaining an understanding that if they field a batted ball they should try to throw it to first base before the runner gets there.

Because games don't offer many learning opportunities, it stands to reason that even at the youngest ages practices are extremely important. Practices, if handled correctly, provide the opportunity to interact with players individually or in small groups, to develop individual motor skills, to teach the basic rules of the game, and to develop an understanding of what it means to be part of a team. As we stated earlier, there's no reason practices can't be as much fun, or even more fun, than games.

Kids are always going to look forward to games. Even the youngest players look forward to their games, although many of the contests are not particularly well organized. At that level it's the parents who seem to lose their patience faster when games are not particularly exciting or enjoyable. Competition drives all of us, no matter what age we are. As kids get older, the games become more fun and exciting for them and their parents. If we can make sure that baseball practices are organized, enjoyable, and effective (so that players look forward to the idea of just being on the field at any time), we'll be making tremendous progress toward our goal of promoting the game of baseball and returning it to its former status. Ultimately, we hope to dive into the concept of developing formal, mandatory training and educational programs for baseball coaches. Until then, we hope that this book is used as a valuable resource by youth baseball coaches everywhere. The rest of this chapter is dedicated to the basic concepts that can help coaches of all ages run effective baseball practices.

Use Small Groups and Stations

It's twice as easy and productive to work with a group of 6 or 7 rather than an entire team of 12 or 15. Likewise, it's easier and more productive to work with a group of 3 instead of a group of 6. We have been running camps with up to 250 kids each since 1999, and one thing that we've learned is that to teach baseball effectively you must make the practices as interactive as possible by using a variety of drills or stations and breaking big groups into smaller groups.

The key is to develop stations that cover the age-appropriate instructional goals we discussed in chapter 3. It's important to understand that attention spans vary according to age level, so the length of each station should be set with an eye toward how long you'll be able to hold your kids' attention. After a few productive minutes, groups should rotate to a new drill or station. It also is important to keep the drills and stations creative. By simply turning a basic drill into a game or contest, you can maintain a child's attention for much longer periods of time. Be careful about having a winner and loser, though, because this can lead to hurt feelings and disappointment. When possible, make all the kids feel like winners, even if this means giving each of them some type of reward at the end of a drill or practice.

Sample Practice Plan—
Ages 12 and Under

10 min.   **Baserunning**

  • Big League Baserunning or dynamic warm-up

20 min.   **Stretch and throw**

  • Stretch around mound or in center field

  • Go over practice plan in detail

45 min.   **Practice in stations (small groups),
15 minutes per station and rotate**

  • Hitting station (one player hits on the field,
    others do tee work and soft toss utilizing
    fences or backstop)

  • Fielding and throwing station (during live
    batting practice)

  • Fly ball and throwing station (during live
    batting practice)

10 min.   **Baserunning**

As always, common sense should prevail. For ages 4 to 6, a practice shouldn't last much longer than an hour. Times should be shortened accordingly if kids are struggling and don't seem to want to be there that day. Practice can be extended at this age group, but only if players ask to stay longer.

Players ages 7 to 9 should be able to handle an hour just about any day and might even be able to maintain interest and concentration for as long as 90 minutes. Try to keep practice to about an hour and 15 minutes for this age group.

Players in the 10-to-12 age group can probably handle 90 minutes with regularity. Use this framework as a guideline and customize practices to fit your needs. You'll find more-detailed practice plans broken down by age group later on in this book.

Sample Practice Plan—Ages 13 and Up

20 min.   **Stretch, run, throw**

20 min.   **Ground balls and fly balls**
(use buckets and systems to minimize throws and maximize repetitions)

- Not taking infield
- Two infield fungo stations
- One outfield fungo station

20 min.   **Team fundamentals**

- Bunt defenses
- First-and-third defenses
- Cutoffs and relays
- Pickoffs and rundowns
- Team baserunning plays

60 min.   **Team batting practice**
(4 stations, 15 minutes each, or 4 stations, 10 minutes each if you want to do another team fundamental)

- Stations can be rotated daily; always include free hitting

Once the season has started, coaches should prioritize which issues need to be addressed during team fundamental sessions. Another team fundamental session can be added, reducing batting practice by 20 minutes. Please note that the infield fungo station does not mean taking a full infield. Batting practice provides opportunities for pitchers to throw on the side and do their running.

Because creating two or three small groups is an important aspect of running an effective, enjoyable practice, it stands to reason that communicating effectively with parents is imperative when attempting to follow this model. We discussed earlier the importance of having someone available to supervise each group. That's one reason the preseason meeting with parents is essential. If you can get a rotation set up so that one or two parents attend each practice, it becomes much easier to run a well-organized, effective, and fun practice.

Let Players Determine Practice Length

Let the kids determine the length of practice. Most youth leagues schedule practices in one-hour time blocks, which might turn out to be way too long for T-ballers or a little too short for 12-year-olds. Regardless, you'll be able to tell by the kids' body language and ability to pay attention when a practice has run its course.

We feel strongly that practices for players aged 10 and younger should last not much longer than an hour. For the youngest players the limit might be 30 or 45 minutes. Obviously, if practices are more fun and interactive with a variety of activities, it will be easier to maintain the team's attention for a full hour. In fact, you'll find that sometimes the kids will be excited and will want to stay longer. That's fine, too, as long as the players dictate that. Other times you might find that after a certain point practice has become unproductive. As coaches, we need to be able to sense this and be willing to cut a practice short. Always keep the big picture in mind. At the end of the season we want the kids' memories of the entire season to be positive. We don't want them to look back and remember that practices were long and tedious.

As players get older, their passion for the game and attention spans are likely to increase. It is okay to adjust practice times accordingly. Again, the key is to be able to read the players and understand when enough is enough. Practices for younger players should accentuate fun, with shorter stations (they love baserunning) and more games and contests.

Players in the 7-to-9 age group will begin to learn team concepts, which can take more time. However, the amount of time spent on these should be limited. If players don't understand something after a certain period of time, they probably aren't going to get it that day.

Move on to something else. Practices for players in this age group should still be limited to about an hour, although some teams will be able to handle more. Let the kids dictate this.

As players continue to get older, team fundamentals and drills become more important. However, remember that throwing, catching, and hitting are the basic fundamental building blocks of the game and should be practiced every day. To accomplish all of this, practices will need to be longer. Even so, coaches should monitor their players to make sure they're not losing their attention by practicing too much. Limiting practices to 90 minutes is a good starting point for teams in the 10-to-12 age group.

Even as players progress up the ranks into high school, coaches need to monitor practice length. Practices for teams at any level shouldn't last much beyond two hours. Coaches of older and more advanced players will spend more time on team fundamentals, such as bunt defenses, cutoffs and relays, first-and-third defenses, and communication. But keep in mind that spending too much time on team fundamentals can be counterproductive. If your players haven't caught on after about 20 minutes, they probably won't get it that day.

Warm-Up

Many times a coach will show up and immediately tell the team to run around the soccer goalposts and come back. As players get older, they begin to understand that this is a warm-up. They know what it means to jog and get loose. Younger players usually don't grasp this concept. They'll view the run as a race and will run as hard as they can in an effort to finish first. Some players won't be able to complete the run at this pace and will tire quickly. Others will push themselves to the very end and exhaust their energy. Either way, you're going to have a bunch of tired kids. It might take them 10 minutes or longer to recover, which is not a good situation when only an hour is allotted for practice.

A better idea for the younger ages is to begin practice with baserunning. Kids love to run bases. In fact, they love it so much you can both begin and end practice with baserunning. We have a drill we really like called Big League Baserunning. The players run from home to first as if they're trying to beat out an infield hit. We stress the concepts of touching the front of the bag and running through the base. Next, players run from first to third. After that, they walk or jog home, and then they run to second base as if they've hit a double. Then they simulate scoring on a hit from second base. Then, if they're not too tired, they can run out a triple or a home run. Each time specific baserunning

Let the Kids
Determine the Outcome

Cal Ripken, Jr.

Youth baseball coaches at all levels should be careful not to insert themselves into the game. As coaches, we have to remember that the game is for the kids. We have a responsibility to teach them the game's rules, fundamentals, and strategies during practices, preparing them for what they'll face in game situations.

And while it's a coach's responsibility to manage a game in terms of playing time, position assignments, and strategies employed, it's important to let the kids and what happens on the field determine the outcome. Most coaches, actually most people in general, are competitive by nature. When game time comes, coaches must remember that their actions can have a tremendous influence on the members of both teams.

Not too long ago, my son Ryan was playing in a national tournament with his 12-year-old travel team. During one of the games Ryan was pitching pretty well, and the game remained close into the late innings. Ryan had been pitching the same way throughout the game and had been giving the opposing batters fits.

As the game wore on, the tension grew on both sides of the field. The game entered the later innings, and Ryan was still cruising. That's when things got interesting. Ryan had been pitching the same way all along, but the opposing coach decided that he was going to alert the home plate umpire to the fact that Ryan was actually lifting his foot up and losing contact with the rubber before pivoting on his delivery to the plate.

By letter of the law this is a balk (the pivot foot must remain in contact with the rubber from the time the pitching motion begins until the ball is released), but we all know that the pitching mounds most youth games are played on are far beneath professional standards. Kids get used to playing on substandard fields where they have to pick their foot up and then put it down because they are dropping down into a hole.

The spirit behind the balk rule is to prevent the pitcher from gaining a competitive advantage through some act of deception. Ryan was not gaining any competitive advantage from what he was doing. More important, he had pitched that way since the beginning of the game. The coach decided he would try to play mind games with a young pitcher to try to get him off of his game and give his team an advantage at a crucial time.

I imagine that any adult could find a way to rattle a youth pitcher mentally. But what does it prove to use that ability to benefit your team? When this happens, the coach has fallen victim to his or her competitive nature, which means that winning has become more important than the overall experience of the kids.

Youth baseball doesn't exist for frustrated adult athletes to impose their wills on young people in an effort to satisfy their own need to succeed athletically. It exists so that players can develop their skills and experience all of the great lessons that can be taught through competing. This does include winning and winning graciously. It also includes losing and losing with dignity. It includes handling smaller successes and failures within the boundaries of acceptable behavior. It does not include intimidation or other tactics employed by coaches to gain a competitive advantage. Remember your responsibilities as a coach and that you are shaping the minds of our future baseball coaches.

fundamentals are stressed. You can even start out with a slow jog, playing follow the leader with a coach, all the way around the bases before moving into Big League Baserunning or a similar activity.

As players get older (over 13), the concept of a dynamic warm-up, including jogging, running, bounding, skipping, and high-knee running, can be introduced and explained. (Younger kids can do the same warm-up, but you usually don't need to tell them why they're doing it.) Older players should be able to arrive at practice and start this type of warm-up as a team on their own before beginning a daily stretching routine.

Cold muscles should never be stretched, but it's important to introduce a stretching routine to any age group. Generating a flow of blood to the muscles before stretching helps prevent injury. Get players' heart rates up and have them start sweating a little bit. After the baserunning or dynamic warm-up, players can sit in a circle to begin their stretching routine. Younger players won't have a real physical need to stretch. They roll out of bed and are loose and ready to go. There's not much danger of them pulling muscles. However, understanding the importance of stretching and developing a routine will help them later, so the earlier the concept of proper stretching is introduced, the better. Team stretching also gives coaches an opportunity to go over the practice plan that has been developed for that day, which reduces wasted time once the practice begins.

Have a Plan

As we mentioned in chapter 1, coaches need to spend some time in advance putting the day's practice on paper. It's even better if this plan can be e-mailed to all players and parents the night before practice. If the coach comes to practice with a plan and can communicate and organize it effectively while the team stretches, the confidence level of the players and parents will increase, and practice will run more efficiently. Team members will understand that the coach is taking his or her responsibilities seriously and is attempting to make the experience as rewarding as possible for all involved. Players are more likely to give maximum effort and attention to a coach who is organized, and parents are less likely to question an organized, dedicated coach. If the coach is disorganized, the players will quickly sense that the coach doesn't really care, which will make it difficult for the coach to run an effective practice and might have a negative impact on the entire season.

Adjust to Limited Field Space

It's very easy for us to tell coaches not to fall into the trap of running a practice where one kid is hitting and everyone else is standing around in the field. After all, we have access to a one-of-a-kind youth baseball academy with eight fields, a synthetic turf practice infield, and multiple batting cages. Most coaches come to practice and have use of one field for an hour. Some coaches don't even get to use a field with a backstop. Those circumstances make it difficult to plan an effective practice. Difficult, but not impossible. You just have to get a little creative.

You can set up batting practice so that players are working at several different stations at the same time. Let's say you have a team of 15 players, which you break into three groups of 5. One group goes to the outfield, where a coach or volunteer hits or throws fly balls and ground balls to players between pitches. Another group goes to the infield, where a coach or volunteer hits or rolls ground balls to players between pitches. The third group is a hitting and baserunning group. One player goes to first base and simulates situational baserunning (seeing a bunt hit the ground before breaking, hit and run, advancing on a hit, reading a fly ball, and so on.). Another player is hitting at home plate (two bunts, two hit and runs, 10 swings). The other three players are hitting plastic, rubber, or foam balls off a tee or doing a soft toss drill into the backstop or a fence. (Don't hit hard baseballs into a fence!)

In this scenario, players are working on hitting, throwing, and catching. If you spend 15 minutes on warming up, throwing, and catching before starting batting practice, you can then let the groups hit for 10 to 15 minutes each and still accomplish quite a bit. There might even be time left at the end to go over a team fundamental for older groups or to do more baserunning or have skills contests for younger teams.

This is just one example of how to make efficient use of limited field space to run an effective practice. Another way is to purchase some portable pop-up nets. These screens are light and fold up into a bag. You can take them anywhere and set them up in a matter of minutes, allowing you to create your own hitting stations under virtually any conditions. Various types of foam rubber balls with raised seams exist and can be used to be used to take safe batting practice almost anywhere. A product that we have developed uses durable small plastic balls with holes and raised seams that are perfect for hitting drills and hold up even when struck with aluminum bats. For more information on these products, see the resources section at the end of the book.

Perfect Practice Makes Perfect

We've all heard that practice makes perfect, but this is not really true. If you practice a skill over and over again the *wrong* way, you're going to perform the skill wrong during a game. Our dad, Cal Ripken, Sr., who played, coached, and managed in the Baltimore Orioles' organization for nearly 40 years, was famous for saying, "Perfect practice makes perfect." He also used to say, "If it's worth doing, it's worth doing right." Both of these sayings reflect the idea that we tend to play the way we practice. In the rest of this book you'll find drills and ideas that provide fun, creative ways to ensure that your players are able to properly practice all the fundamentals they need for success on the baseball field.

We're going to arm you with a plan and a knowledge base in the fundamentals that will allow you to make baseball a positive experience for your entire team. By understanding and applying the concept of small groups and stations, your players will get more repetitions in a shorter period of time, increasing the efficiency of your practices. Players will stay active throughout practice without getting bored, and they'll begin to understand the importance of completing tasks the right way every time so that they carry good habits into game situations.

We want players to be disciplined and practice the right way every time so that their reaction to situations during games becomes automatic. Although we want them to understand discipline and the importance of approaching practice in a certain way, we still want them to have fun. So, be creative. Introduce new twists to our drills. Turn the drills into contests. Give out prizes to those who practice best. Never lose sight of the fact that baseball is a game that should be fun for both players and coaches. If the game ceases to be fun, you need to take a step back and revaluate your approach.

PART II

Teaching the Ripken Way

5

Hitting and Baserunning Drills

Somebody somewhere comes up with a new baseball drill every day. Guaranteed. We have found that many of the new, sometimes complicated, drills that pop up all the time are simply variations of the basic drills for hitting, throwing, and fielding that have been passed down from generation to generation. Instead of jumping on the bandwagon and continuing to unveil fancy or unique drills, we have held to our philosophy of keeping things simple.

When we say "keep it simple," we don't mean things must be elementary or plain. When we began our camps we used just a few simple drills, and the feedback we got from participants and parents was overwhelmingly positive. Since then we have taken those core fundamental drills, added a few twists, gotten creative to make some of them more exciting and keep them interesting for kids.

In all, we have implemented more than 50 drills that cover the basic fundamentals we teach. Sure, some of them are for players who are a little older or more advanced, but few of the drills are too complicated for even the youngest of players to at least understand. What follows in this chapter are offensive drills we've developed that can help you make your players better while keeping practice fun.

At the beginning of part III, you will discover a Practice Planner, which is essentially a menu of drills grouped by age appropriateness. When you get to the chapters in part III that provide practice plans, the drills will be referenced by their groupings there as well to make it easy for you to find them in the Practice Planner and then to locate their descriptions. Remember that our practice plans are there to give you an idea of what drills fit where. As your players progress, you'll want to substitute different drills to allow for further skill development. Try to stay within your age group when selecting drills until you're certain that your team has accomplished its five goals. Some teams will do this more quickly than others. It's at that point that you might want to think about adding some of the more advanced drills. Be careful, though. You don't want to frustrate your players by having them attempt drills they're not physically or mentally prepared for yet.

Hitting Drills

Many coaches feel that once they're on the baseball field they have to be teaching. Yes, teaching kids how to play baseball is a primary part of a youth coach's job description, but learning how to observe first is just as important. You can't see a young player hit for the first time and immediately start teaching. Before any instruction can take place, you must observe the player's approach and analyze the results. You might see a hitter swing once and believe that you notice two or three components of the swing that should be adjusted. What happens if you help the player make those adjustments and suddenly he or she can't hit anything? Watch a player hit for an extended period of time and at first resist the urge to teach. If the results are consistently good, hold your thoughts until a time when the player is struggling and needs advice.

When you do get the opportunity to instruct your hitters, resist the urge to do so when the players are taking batting practice or hitting in game situations. Some say that hitting a baseball is the most difficult skill to master in all of sports. A pitcher is throwing a round, hard ball as fast as he or she can at the batter, changing speeds and making the ball dive, dip, and dance. The batter is standing there with a round bat and a coach telling him or her to hit that round ball squarely. Sound tough? Well, it's definitely not easy. But it's even more difficult when the batter has a whirlwind of instructions he or she is trying to remember and follow as the ball leaves the pitcher's hand. Stride toward the pitcher! Keep your hands up! Squash the bug! Keep your weight back! And so on. This type of advice can paralyze a young hitter.

Once again, in batting practice and game situations, the coach needs to observe first and teach later. Make mental notes or write down what each player needs to work on, and then find the drill in this section that best suits the problem. When it comes to hitting, all teaching should be done during practice time when players are working on drills and not during free hitting or games.

K E Y   P O I N T S

1. Stance—starting point; need vision, balance, and plate coverage.

2. Grip—loose grip in the fingers with the "door knocking" knuckles lined up to unlock the wrists and allow for greater bat speed.

3. Weight shift—weight shifts to backside, gathering energy, before being taken forward; verbal cue: "You have to go back to go forward."

4. Stride—short and soft, toward the pitcher.

5. Swing—short and quick, using hands, wrists, and forearms.

6. Follow-through—one or two hands; takes care of itself if all other elements of swing are in place.

5.1 Free Hitting

Age Appropriate

Grouping 1, all ages

Objective

To let players hit free from coaching or instruction, allowing them to put all of the pieces of the swing together after drill work

Setup

Bucket of balls, coach or pitcher to throw or to feed a pitching machine

Execution

This is what we call regular batting practice or live hitting in the cage. Let players hit and have fun. Resist the urge to coach. Coaching and tinkering are for drill work. As players get older it's okay to have them work on bunting, hit and runs, and moving runners over during free hitting or batting practice. Hitting is supposed to be fun, so let the kids have at it. Note when corrections are needed and work on them during drill sessions.

Goalie Game

5.2

Age Appropriate

Grouping 2, ages 4 to 9

Objective

To work on hitting the ball where it's pitched, developing bat control, and creating a short swing to improve contact

Setup

Home plate in front of a hockey or lacrosse goal, pitching machine or tennis ball machine, bucket of balls

Execution

Set up a hockey or lacrosse goal as a backstop with a home plate in front of the net. Use a pitching machine that throws softer balls or use a tennis ball machine to throw balls toward the goal. The batter tries to keep balls from going into the goal by swinging at the pitches. The coach can throw harder than normal if machines are not available.

5.3 Hitting Contests

Age Appropriate
Grouping 1, all ages

Objective
To add a competitive angle to regular hitting drills to make them seem less like work

Setup
Depends on the drill; usually a bucket of balls and a coach or pitching machine to feed or pitch

Execution
Almost any hitting drill can be turned into a contest using a point system. Award a point for a hard ground ball up the middle, 2 points for a line drive up the middle, and 5 points for a line drive up the middle that reaches the back wall of a cage or the outfield grass (depending on where you're hitting). Develop your own point systems for whatever concept you're teaching. Stress proper hitting mechanics at all times. The scoring sheet included here is designed to help you track individual and group totals for two rounds as well as the team total. Keep a record and compare results over the season to see how your team is progressing.

Player/group	Round 1	Round 2	Total
_____	_____	_____	_____
_____	_____	_____	_____
_____	_____	_____	_____
_____	_____	_____	_____
_____	_____	_____	_____
_____	_____	_____	_____
_____	_____	_____	_____
_____	_____	_____	_____
_____	_____	_____	_____
_____	_____	_____	_____

Group 1 total _____   *Group 3 total* _____
Group 2 total _____   *Team total* _____

Knock Out the Catcher

5.4

Age Appropriate
Grouping 2, ages 4 to 9

Objective
To work on hitting the ball hard up the middle by keeping the front shoulder in and striding toward the pitcher

Setup
A coach, catcher's gear, a bucket of soft or sponge rubber balls, a stool or bucket to sit on

Execution
A coach dresses in full catcher's gear and sits on a chair 10 to 15 feet from home plate. The coach tosses the ball and tells the hitter to knock him off the chair. Without really knowing it, players are working on hitting the ball hard up the middle.

(continued)

5.4 Knock Out the Catcher *(continued)*

 Coaching Keys

Because this drill is intended for younger players, you don't want to get too technical here. However, if players are really struggling to hit the ball up the middle and are pulling weak ground balls, they are probably "pulling off" the ball. This means that they are likely stepping and taking the front shoulder away from the pitcher. To correct this, you can toss the ball more to the outside part of the plate and force the stride and shoulder to come more toward the pitcher.

Line Drive Home Run Derby

5.5

Age Appropriate

Grouping 3, ages 4 to 12

Objective

To work on keeping the head, eyes, and shoulders as level as possible throughout the swing; hitting line drives

Setup

Bucket of soft or sponge rubber baseballs, home plate, hitting net for a backstop, pitching machine (optional)

Execution

Use soft or sponge rubber baseballs and set up in the outfield, hitting toward the fence. Pitch overhand or toss balls underhand to players and award points for hard ground balls and line drives. Home runs count 5 points if they are line drives. High fly balls are outs, even if they travel beyond the fence. Swings and misses, pop-ups, and foul balls are outs. Give each player 3 outs and see who scores the most points. This drill can be done just as well with a pitching machine. The scoring sheet below will help you keep track of individual, group, and team scores. Analyze your team's progress by comparing results throughout the season.

Player/group	Round 1	Round 2	Total
_____	_____	_____	_____
_____	_____	_____	_____
_____	_____	_____	_____
_____	_____	_____	_____
_____	_____	_____	_____
_____	_____	_____	_____
_____	_____	_____	_____
_____	_____	_____	_____
_____	_____	_____	_____
_____	_____	_____	_____
_____	_____	_____	_____

Group 1 total _____   *Group 3 total* _____
Group 2 total _____   *Team total* _____

5.6

Tee Hitting for Distance

Age Appropriate
Grouping 1, all ages

Objective
To show how a good weight shift can generate power and that a level or slightly downward swing is best for driving the ball farther

Setup
Batting tee, bucket of balls, players in the field (optional), cones, markers, or stakes (optional)

Execution
Players use proper fundamentals to see how far they can hit a ball off of a tee from home plate. Use weight shift ("go back to go forward"), winding up almost like a pitcher to take the weight to the back side before exploding forward. The head should stay on the ball. The front shoulder and stride should go directly toward the pitcher until contact is made. Batters who drop the back shoulder and try to intentionally hit the ball high are eliminated. Line drives are best, but hard ground balls count. Have players run out and stand next to their best hits or mark them with stakes.

 Coaching Keys

Any time young players hit off a tee, especially if you tell them that they're hitting for distance, they'll tend to drop the back shoulder and swing with a visible uppercut. If players are hitting under the ball and getting a chunk of the tee with their swings or topping ground balls, the back shoulder dropping is likely the cause. Explain to them that the high fly balls they hit by doing this are really just pop-ups, not home runs, and that by swinging down and taking that barrel of the bat straight to the ball they will hit harder line drives and fly balls that will turn into home runs as they get bigger and stronger.

a

b

c

5.7 Soft Toss

Age Appropriate
Grouping 1, all ages

Objective
To use a proper grip and understand how that helps improve bat speed; verbal cue: "Loose hands, quick bat"

Setup
Bucket of balls, coach, player or toss machine to toss; net, screen, or fence to hit into

Execution
This is a standard hitting drill that can be done virtually anywhere. Teammates can toss to one another, or a coach can toss to a player. The batter takes his or her stance; the tosser kneels across from the hitter, slightly in front of home plate in foul ground, not in the direction that the ball will be hit. The ball is tossed underhand so the batter can hit it out in front of the plate. The hitter wants to concentrate on having a loose grip in the fingers with the "door knocking" knuckles lined up. This will allow the wrists to unlock, promoting a quicker swing using the hands, wrists, and forearms. Batters should think *loose hands, quick bat.* This drill works best if done into a screen with a target, but it can also be done into a fence if plastic balls, tennis balls, or rubber balls are used. Never hit baseballs into a fence.

 Coaching Keys

If players seem to be getting jammed quite a bit, take a look at where the tosses are coming from and are being hit. A lot of coaches try to soft toss from a position directly across from the batter. When the ball is coming directly at the batter, he or she actually has to drag the bat to the ball, hitting it at a location that's not in front of home plate. The toss should come from an angle slightly in front of home plate and be struck slightly in front of the plate. This allows the wrists to unlock and the barrel of the bat to get to the ball.

5.8 Tee Work

Age Appropriate

Grouping 1, all ages

Objective

To develop proper weight shift; verbal cue: "You have to go back to go forward"

Setup

Batting tee, bucket of balls, net, screen, or fence to hit into

Execution

Players adjust the batting tee to a height that makes them swing down slightly to get the barrel of the bat to the ball. Players hit into the screen or a net with a target. Work strictly on weight shift ("Go back to go forward"). Take all the weight to the back side before exploding forward. Keep the head down and eyes on the ball. Take the front foot and front shoulder directly toward pitcher. Try to hit the ball at the target each time. Avoid an uppercut swing. If you don't have a net, plastic balls, tennis balls, or soft rubber balls can be hit into a fence. Never hit baseballs into a fence.

 Coaching Keys

To help keep players from dropping the front shoulder, tell them to focus on hitting the ball into a target directly in front of the tee. If they're pulling the ball weakly, remind them to go straight back first before striding straight forward toward the pitcher ("Go straight back, then straight forward"). If they hit the tee, top ground balls, or swing and miss often, have them pick a spot on the ball and focus on that spot until they make contact.

5.9 Short Toss From the Front

Age Appropriate

Grouping 1, all ages

Objective

To use the big part of the field by keeping the front shoulder in long enough to hit balls tossed to the outside part of the plate up the middle or the opposite way

Setup

L-screen, stool or bucket for coach to sit on, coach to toss, bucket of balls

Execution

This drill stresses using the big part of the field. Coach sits on a bucket or chair behind a screen about 10 to 12 feet out in front of home plate. Coach tosses pitches underhand, but firmly, to outside part of plate. Batter tries to keep the front shoulder in and drive the ball up the middle or the other way. Some batters naturally will pull the pitches, which is okay if that's their natural swing and they hit line drives. Weakly pulled ground balls are what we're trying to avoid.

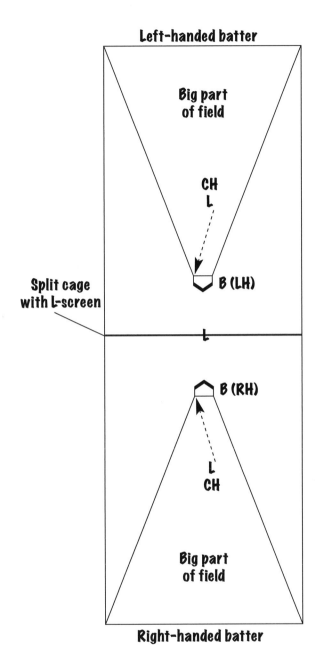

77

5.10 Stickball Drill

Age Appropriate
Grouping 4, ages 7 to 15+

Objective
To develop a quick swing that allows the hitter to maintain balance throughout

Setup
Small plastic balls, coach or player to toss, thin stickball bat, net or screen to hit into

Execution
This drill uses small plastic balls and a shaved-down stickball-type bat. (You can make your own or look in various sporting goods stores for a similar product.) Have the batter take a natural stride and stop without starting the swing. This is the starting point. Take the bottom half of the body out of the drill. The tosser flips the ball to the hitter just as in regular soft toss. Batters swing as hard as they can, maintaining balance without striding, and reload quickly. As soon as they reload, the next ball is tossed. Each hitter should take 5 to 10 swings. This drill is best done into a net or screen. Balls might be too small to hit into a fence. Batters should try to hit every ball into the target. The drill stresses balance. If hitters can't reload quickly or stumble, they are not balanced throughout the swing.

 ### Coaching Keys

If the batter is swinging late and can't seem to get ready for the next pitch, slow down the pace. This is not a race. Let the batter set the pace. If the reason that the batter can't get loaded in time is because he or she is off balance, try having the hitter use a wider or more narrow stance until a comfort zone is located.

5.10

a

b

5.11 Bunting Drill

Age Appropriate
Grouping 1, all ages

Objective
To work on keeping sacrifice bunts away from the pitcher

Setup
Four cones, bucket of balls, coach or player to pitch

Execution
Set up two cones down the first base line about halfway between home plate and the mound. One should be about 3 feet inside the baseline, the other about 8 to 10 feet inside the line toward the mound. The same thing should be done on the third base line. A coach can throw from a shortened distance with players taking turns bunting. The idea is to stop or push the ball between the cones. Try not to make the bunts too perfect. Make the pitcher come off the mound to field the ball. Stress that players pivot both feet instead of squaring to bunt. Have them start with the bat at the top of the strike zone and the barrel of the bat above the hands at an angle, bending their knees for lower pitches and leaving pitches above the hands alone. Players should give with the pitch to deaden the ball and use the bottom hand to guide the bat and push the ball in the desired direction. Give the players five tries each; see how many each one can get between the cones.

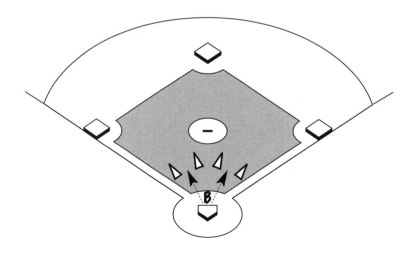

Coaching Keys

If the ball is being popped up quite a bit the barrel of the bat probably is below the hands at the moment of contact. The player may be either bunting a pitch that's too high, starting the bat too low and then bringing it up to meet the ball, or not bending his or her knees to get to lower pitches. If the ball is being bunted consistently back to the pitcher, the batter is not using the lower hand to angle the bat correctly. If the batter is bunting a lot of foul balls, he or she is most likely not placing the bat in front of home plate.

5.12 One-Arm Drill

Age Appropriate
Grouping 5, ages 10 to 15+

Objective
To develop a quick, short swing that takes the bat head on a direct path to the baseball

Setup
L-screen, coach to pitch, bucket or stool to sit on, bucket of balls

Execution
Can be done by players of almost any age once they can make consistent contact with pitched balls. Coach stands or sits about 8 to 10 feet in front of the batter behind a screen. Coach tosses pitches overhand or underhand. Batter hits first five pitches with two hands, then takes the top hand off the bat for the next five pitches. Use normal game bat. Try not to choke up, if possible. Hitters can tuck the elbow into their side for more leverage, if necessary. After hitting five with one hand, hitter finishes up by hitting five more with two hands. One-hand reps should be difficult. This drill should help batters take the bat on a more direct path to the ball. They should feel a difference when hitting the final set of five.

 Coaching Keys

Let batters choke up if they can't control the bat or allow them to tuck the elbow into their side if they're struggling to take the barrel of the bat directly to the ball.

Lob Toss

5.13

Age Appropriate

Grouping 5, ages 10 to 15+

Objective

To keep the weight loaded on the back foot as long as possible before shifting the weight forward to hit; verbal cue: "Let it get deep."

Setup

L-screen, bucket of balls, coach to pitch, bucket or stool to sit on

Execution

This is a drill that Cal worked on every day. Coach sits or stands behind a screen about 20 to 40 feet in front of home plate, depending on the player's ability level and the ability of the coach to throw the ball with accuracy. The coach tosses balls with a high arc (as in slow-pitch softball). The batter lets the ball travel as far as possible (verbal cue: "Let it get deep") before trying to drive the ball. Designed to help hitters be patient and avoid shifting weight to the front foot too soon.

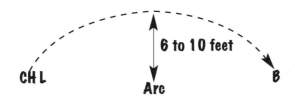

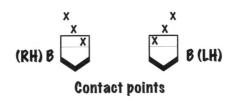

 Coaching Keys

If players can't stay back and consistently shift their weight forward too soon, have them widen their stance and cut down on the length of the stride.

(continued)

a

b

Baserunning Drills

At some point, we're not exactly sure when, baserunning goes from being fun to seeming like work. Baserunning is a valuable and often overlooked part of the game that should be practiced every time a team is on the field. How many times have you heard coaches complain that baserunning mistakes cost their team the game? Most times we would bet that those mistakes were a result of a lack of attention to baserunning in practice.

A team that runs the bases well can really put the pressure on an opposing defense, forcing a team to make quicker decisions than normal. Whenever the decision-making process has to speed up, a team is prone to making defensive mistakes. Good baserunners can help your team manufacture runs and win games even when players are struggling at the plate.

At the youngest ages, baserunning can be used as part of a warm-up and as a fun way to end practice, helping players improve their conditioning in such a way that they aren't even aware of it. As players get older, you can use baserunning drills for conditioning and to reinforce the basic fundamentals that will help your team become better on the basepaths. There are plenty of ways to make baserunning drills fun for older players, too.

5.14 Baserunning Relays

Age Appropriate
Grouping 1, all ages

Objective
To learn how proper turns at each base can help players get to their destination faster

Setup
Field with bases (preferably pegged bases), a stopwatch

Execution
Have groups of two or four players compete by running around the bases to see who can finish with the fastest combined time. One player circles the bases, and then as soon as he or she touches home plate, the next player in the group starts. You'll find that the groups that run the bases the best fundamentally can and will beat the groups with the faster players. You can use cones to show the path for the proper turns at each base.

Big League Baserunning

5.15

Age Appropriate

Grouping 1, all ages

Objective

To work on various baserunning situations and conditioning

Setup

Field with bases (preferably pegged bases)

Execution

Players line up at home plate and run home to first, all the way through the bag. Then they shuffle off of first, take a crossover step and run first to third before jogging to home plate *(a)*. Players line up at home again and run out a double. They then simulate scoring from second on a hit *(b)*. Then have them run out a triple or a home run, if you wish. Emphasis should be on making a proper turn at each base as well as stepping on the inside of the base and using the bag to push off of (like a starting block) toward the next base.

 Coaching Keys

If players are having trouble making correct turns and taking a proper route to the next base, set up cones to mark the proper path. Players will take a path to the outside of the cones.

(continued)

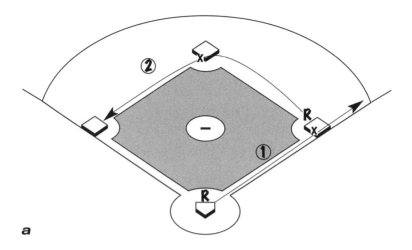

a

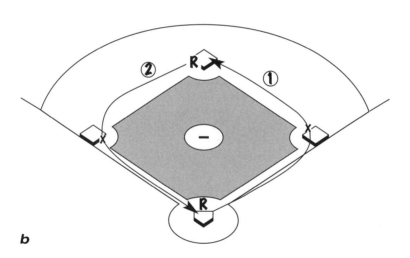

b

Head to Head

5.16

Age Appropriate

Grouping 1, all ages

Objective

To demonstrate that the fastest player isn't always the best baserunner; to understand how to make a proper turn when going from home to second and second to home

Setup

Field with bases (preferably pegged bases)

Execution

One player starts at second, and the other starts at home. The coach stands on pitcher's mound and yells, "Go!" Player from second is simulating scoring on a hit. Player at home simulates running out a double. Whoever gets to his or her destination first wins. Point out players who adhere to proper fundamentals when running the bases well.

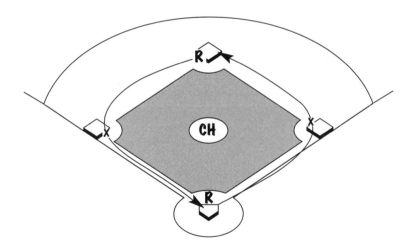

5.17 Slip and Slide

Age Appropriate
Grouping 3, ages 4 to 12

Objective
To develop proper sliding fundamentals in a safe, fun environment

Setup
Slip-and-slide, hose, base to slide into

Execution
Use a slip-and-slide on a soft, grassy surface to illustrate the proper sliding techniques. This is a fun way to show players how to slide without risking cuts and bruises. Place a base at the end of the slip-and-slide. This is a great way to end a hot practice.

 Coaching Keys

Although you should avoid teaching the head-first slide, it can be fun to let players go head first at the end of the drill. If players tend to roll over on their sides when attempting to slide properly, remind them that they must slide on their butts, not on their hips. This will keep their toes pointed up instead of sideways and lower the risk of knee injuries. Their weight can be more on one buttock than the other, but the butt should be in contact with the ground. Have them focus on bent-leg or pop-up slides and hook slides.

6

Throwing and Pitching Drills

Defense in baseball is comprised of two parts: throwing and catching. We always stress that the most succesful teams generally are the ones that play catch the best. So, which component of defense is most important? That's really impossible to say, but one thing is for sure: A player can't catch what he or she can't reach. If a throw is not close enough to a teammate to be caught, an error is sure to occur. The main goal of a defense should be to eliminate the amount of bases given away to the opposing team. Errors lead to free bases, so you can see why accurate throwing is so important.

Throwing Drills

Many coaches take throwing for granted. They tell their teams to play catch as part of their warm-up and then ignore what's going on. Too many young baseball players never learn the proper way to throw, and even when they are told how to throw correctly, they often are never observed while playing catch. The only way that young players are going to build arm strength is by throwing correctly for a defined period of time at every practice. This also is the only way that they are going to develop the muscle memory necessary to throw freely and accurately in game situations.

As with every other fundamental skill in baseball, repetition is the key when it comes to throwing. As our dad often said, "Practice doesn't make perfect; perfect practice makes perfect." If kids throw every day but aren't doing it properly, that will be evident in game situations. Younger players can get bored with playing catch, so we've included some drills in this chapter to keep it interesting for them. Older, more serious players don't seem to mind playing catch, but as they get stronger you'll see them start to use different arm angles and deliveries when warming up. So, the fun drills in this chapter can be done by almost any age group. At all levels, be sure to reinforce the importance of throwing and catching. Monitor your team's progress, even if from a distance, every time your players warm up.

Throwing

KEY POINTS

1. Use a four-seam grip.

2. Take the ball down, out, and up out of the glove (circular motion).

3. Hand above the ball at first, shifting to behind the ball as release point approaches.

4. Elbow above the shoulder.

5. Point front shoulder toward target.

6. Step toward target.

7. Release ball.

8. Follow throw (or follow through).

6.1 Cutoff Relay Race

Age Appropriate
Grouping 1, all ages

Objective
To work on catching with two hands, making a quick transfer, and proper footwork when receiving and making throws

Setup
Bucket of balls, small groups of players

Execution
Create groups of three, four, or five players to race. Players stand in a straight line with the others in their group, beginning at the spot where the ball is picked up, spaced evenly. All groups go at the same time. An outfielder picks up a ball lying on the warning track next to the fence and throws to his first teammate. That teammate turns his body, catches, generates momentum, and throws to the next teammate. This continues until the ball reaches the last player. The team that finishes first wins.

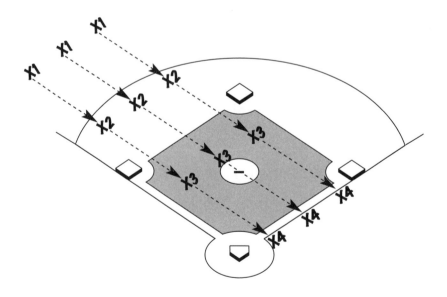

Coaching Keys

The most common problems you'll find when executing relay throws are with kids who turn the wrong way before throwing (they turn toward the throwing side instead of the glove side) and kids who catch the ball flat-footed. Remind these players to turn toward the glove side as the ball approaches and to start moving toward the next target as they receive the ball. When they receive the throw, they'll already be moving in the right direction, so all they'll have to do is throw the ball and follow the throw.

6.2 Long-Toss Golf

Age Appropriate

Grouping 3, ages 4 to 12

Objective

To work on proper long-tossing technique, building arm strength, and throwing accuracy

Setup

Cones (or some other target), balls, paint, or tape

Execution

Place a cone or some other target in the outfield, far enough away to challenge the players' arm strength. Draw, paint, or tape a circle around the target, representing a golf green. Each player tosses a ball toward the target. Points are awarded for landing on the green or hitting the pin. The player coming closest to the pin each round can be awarded bonus points. You can use the same target over and over, make new targets, or set up a course. Limit this drill to between 25 and 50 tosses per player. Perform once per week for younger players.

Coaching Keys

This is a long-toss drill designed to build arm strength, so players should work on throwing the ball with an arc and getting the ball to carry. Young players might tend to throw the ball really high, almost like a pop-up, which won't help their throwing mechanics. All players should use proper throwing mechanics. The player's shoulders should remain almost on the same plane throughout the throwing motion. If the back shoulder is dropping too much, demonstrate the proper technique. Remind players that an accurate one- or two-hop throw is better than a longer throw that's off target.

6.3 Shoot and Score!

Age Appropriate

Grouping 3, ages 4 to 12

Objective

To improve throwing accuracy

Setup

Two goals, a bucket of balls, target (optional)

Execution

After players warm up their arms, set up two goals across from each other at a distance at which they can throw the ball into the goals in the air and on a line. One player stands to the side of each goal. Players take turns trying to throw the ball into the other's goal. Award 1 point for each ball that rolls into the goal and 2 points for a ball that enters the goal in the air. Another variation is to hang, tape, or paint a target onto the goal. Then 1 point is awarded for scoring a goal and 2 points for hitting the target. Targets also can be hung on fences, soccer goals, or walls. Hold a team competition to see who throws most accurately.

 Coaching Keys

Players who miss the target usually aren't stepping toward the target or aren't pointing the front shoulder toward the target.

Throw for Distance

6.4

Age Appropriate

Grouping 2, ages 4 to 9

Objective

To learn how using the body's momentum can help you throw the ball farther

Setup

Football field (or other marked field); a bucket of balls; cones, stakes, or other markers (optional)

Execution

If you practice near a football field, have players line up at the goal line one at a time. Stress proper mechanics and have each player throw a ball (or several balls) to see who can set the "world record." After a few rounds, have players shuffle their feet and follow their throws so they can see the results of generating momentum toward their target. You can disqualify players who don't use proper mechanics. Celebrate world records as well as throws made using proper mechanics. This drill is a fun way to build arm strength through long tossing and to emphasize the importance of mechanics and footwork. This drill should be done only once a week. Have younger players line up on a line (foul line or goal line) and throw at the same time. They can then run to their ball, see whose ball went farthest, pick it up, and run back.

 Coaching Keys

This is a long-toss drill that's also used to help players learn to use their bodies to throw the ball farther. Remember that the shoulders should remain on almost the same plane throughout the throwing motion and that players should not throw pop-ups. Try to limit the number of shuffles a player takes to simulate how quickly they should get rid of the ball in a game situation. Usually, no more than two shuffle-steps should be taken.

6.5 Twenty-One

Age Appropriate
Grouping 1, all ages

Objective
To improve throwing accuracy

Setup
Two players and a baseball

Execution
This is a game played by baseball players at all levels. As players play catch, 1 point is awarded to the thrower for each ball caught at chest level. Two points are awarded for a ball caught at head level. Points can be deducted for uncatchable throws. If a throw is accurate but the receiver misses it, points are still awarded to the thrower. The first player to 21 wins. Stress proper mechanics. Set up a team competition in which winners move on and losers are eliminated. To speed things up, play to 15 instead of 21.

Other Throwing Games

6.6

Age Appropriate
Grouping 1, all ages

Objective
To make basic throwing drills more fun

Setup
A bucket of balls and a target

Execution
Just about any throwing drill can be turned into a contest by adding a target. Players can throw at a painted, taped, or drawn target on a fence, wall, or screen. Or they can try to knock a ball off a batting tee. Try anything that makes players concentrate and attempt to throw with accuracy. Stress proper mechanics at all times: four-seam grip; get the ball down, out, and up; elbow above the shoulder; point the front shoulder; step toward the target; follow the throw.

Coaching Keys

When players are struggling with their accuracy, check for a proper four-seam grip, that the front shoulder points toward the target, that the step is toward the target, and that the elbow is staying above the shoulder. Remind players to follow their throws toward the target after releasing the ball.

(continued)

Throwing and Pitching Drills

As is true of hitting, a coach can't just walk onto a field, watch a kid throw a couple of pitches, and immediately start correcting mechanical flaws. Be patient and use your observational skills before teaching. You might have a pitcher who throws using a three-quarter delivery and want to change that right away. But what if that pitcher throws really hard, is consistently in the strike zone, and generates good movement with each pitch? As long as that player keeps his or her elbow above the shoulder, which is a key to preventing elbow injuries, you don't want to mess with success.

Instead of making a knee-jerk reaction after seeing a young player throw a couple of pitches, observe the pitcher over time. If the player is old enough and strong enough, ask him or her to throw all of his or her pitches and make notes about everything you see. Then, after careful observation, decide which of the drills that follow might help your pitcher improve his or her mechanics. Many of the drills you will find in this section can be used to help young players who are having problems with their basic throwing mechanics.

When it comes to pitching we have a saying, "You learn to throw hard by throwing hard." Young pitchers should throw a lot of fastballs—four-seamers and two-seamers—to build arm strength. Players of just about any age can learn how to throw a change-up, too, once their hands become big enough. But even these players should throw almost all fastballs in games and practices. At some point you can introduce to a young pitcher the correct way to throw breaking balls. Allow him or her to try only the correct method in practice. If he or she can throw a breaking pitch correctly and generate some movement, you might want to allow him or her to throw one or two per inning in game situations.

If a player gets a considerable amount of movement on the ball but doesn't throw the breaking pitch properly, resist the urge to allow him or her to throw that pitch in games. Can he or she get people out with it? Sure. But allowing young pitchers to throw breaking balls incorrectly can lead to arm problems down the road. Perhaps even more important, if young pitchers rely too much on breaking balls, they won't develop the arm strength they need to improve the velocity on their fastball. As these pitchers progress to the high school ranks, other pitchers who have focused on throwing fastballs and building arm strength will pass them by. Pitchers who have thrown a lot of fastballs will be able to throw harder *and* they'll have a better breaking ball, because their arm strength will have developed properly.

Also, don't forget the importance of pitchers learning how to field their position. Included in this section you'll find pitcher's fielding practice (PFP) drills that work well for pitchers of all ages.

Pitching

K E Y   P O I N T S

Focus on the five key links in the pitching chain:

1. Feet—take a small step back with nonthrowing-side foot, keeping the weight over the stationary foot, which is turned parallel and touching the rubber.

2. Balance position—nonthrowing-side leg comes up, glove is at waist level, torso is slightly forward so that the weight is centered over the pivot foot.

3. Power position—hand above the ball, take the ball down out of the glove and up (circular motion) as the front foot strides toward home plate.

4. Rotation—hand goes from above the ball to behind it as the release point is approached; elbow is above the shoulder.

5. Follow-through—end up in a good fielding position; the follow-through takes care of itself if mechanics are correct; don't be too picky about a perfect follow-though if the results are consistent.

One-Knee Drill

6.7

Age Appropriate

Grouping 1, all ages

Objective

To introduce players to proper throwing mechanics, particularly arm action (getting the ball down, out, and up)

Setup

Two players (or a player and a coach) and a baseball

Execution

This drill breaks down the player's arm action and works on keeping the elbow at the proper level. Players drop their throwing-side knee to the ground with the opposite knee up and play catch at a short distance using a four-seam grip to throw. Concentrate on taking the ball down, out, and up from the glove and keeping the elbow above the shoulder. The hand is on top of the ball as it's taken out of the glove, shifting to behind the ball as the arm comes forward. Players don't throw hard. Have them check their grip, hand, and elbow position after bringing the ball down out and up. Hand should be on top of the ball with fingers pointing away from the target just before the arm comes forward. From there, the player points the front shoulder toward the target, rotates the hips, brings the arm forward, and releases the ball, keeping the elbow above the shoulder. Younger players can use soft baseballs or do this drill with their coaches.

 Coaching Keys

Many young players turn their hand so that it's under the ball before they bring the arm forward. Some people call this "pie throwing." Think of how you have to hold a pie to throw it at someone; the palm is facing up so that you don't drop the pie. This is the opposite of how you should throw a baseball. For players who do this, have them stop their motion just before they bring the arm forward and check to see that the hand is on top of the ball and that the ball is pointing straight back. Other players will let their elbows drop below shoulder level at the release point. To fix this problem, try the Tee Drill (next).

(continued)

Tee Drill

6.8

Age Appropriate
Grouping 4, ages 7 to 15+

Objective
To help players learn to keep the elbow above the shoulder when throwing

Setup
Two players (or a player and a coach), batting tee, a baseball

Execution
This drill helps prevent players from dropping their elbow when throwing. Players assume a one-knee position, as described in the One-Knee Drill. A batting tee is placed on the throwing side, close enough so that if the elbow drops it hits the tee. Players take the ball down, out, and up—checking their grip as necessary before rotating forward and releasing the ball. The presence of the tee will force players to consciously think about not dropping the elbow below shoulder level. Over time this will develop muscle memory that leads to proper throwing mechanics.

6.9 Power Position Drill

Age Appropriate

Grouping 1, all ages

Objective

To develop a proper grip and arm action

Setup

Two players (or a player and a coach), baseballs, a pitching mound (optional).

Execution

Variations of this drill can be done at all levels. The drill can be simplified for the youngest age groups to stress which direction to face when throwing; the proper four-seam grip; getting the ball down, out, and up; keeping the hand above the ball prior to rotation; keeping the elbow above the shoulder; pointing the front shoulder toward the target; stepping toward the target; and following through. For older and more advanced players, the drill can help troubleshoot mechanical problems often experienced by pitchers. Players create a wide base with their feet and hold the ball with a four-seam grip. Weight shifts to the backside before moving forward. Hands break, and the weight goes back. Power position is assumed (check as necessary): hand above the ball with fingers pointed away from the target. Weight is back; elbow is above the shoulder. Front shoulder points toward the target. Hand shifts from above the ball to behind the ball as the arm moves forward through rotation. Ball is released (does not have to be thrown hard). Follow-through takes place with the trail foot staying in contact with the rubber. Players rotate on the back foot so the hips turn. Front toe points forward.

 Coaching Keys

The Power Position Drill can be used to troubleshoot the following mechanical flaws:

Short-arming. Start in the finish position with the throwing arm extended forward as if following through. Take weight all the way back through the power position before finishing to stretch out the throwing motion.

Getting pitches up. Have the catcher shorten up with the pitcher throwing from a mound. To throw downhill from the power position, the pitcher must get the elbow up and stay on top of the ball.

Long-striders. Again, have the catcher shorten up with the pitcher throwing from a mound. If the stride is too long the pitcher won't be able to compensate to get downhill in time to throw a strike.

Breaking balls or off-speed pitches. Between starts, pitchers struggling with their grips, mechanics, or control can practice their breaking balls and off-speed pitches from the power position on or off a mound from a shortened distance to get a better feel and make corrections.

6.9

6.10 Long Toss

Age Appropriate
Grouping 4, ages 7 to 15+

Objective
To develop arm strength and lengthen the throwing motion

Setup
Two players and a baseball

Execution
This drill helps improve any player's arm strength and is not just for pitchers. Warm up playing catch. Once the arm is warm, move back a few steps with each throw. Get far enough apart that it's a challenge to get the ball to the partner. Take a long step forward, concentrate on keeping the elbow way above the shoulder, and throw the ball with a slight arc. Shoulders should remain on about the same plane throughout the delivery; we're not trying to throw pop-ups. It's okay if the ball arrives on one hop. Throw until arms start to fatigue, then move closer to finish up. Pitchers should do this drill between starts. Younger players shouldn't try the drill more than once a week. Older position players can do it several times a week.

Balance Position Drill

6.11

Age Appropriate

Grouping 4, ages 7 to 15+

Objective

To help players understand how to gather energy at balance position before exploding toward the plate

Setup

Pitcher, catcher, pitching mound (optional), a baseball

Execution

Pitcher throws from a mound to a catcher at a shortened distance. Start motion from the stretch, lifting the leg and pausing for a 3-count (one, one thousand; two, one thousand; three, one thousand) at balance position (upper and lower body come together, leg slightly closed with butt cheek pointing toward catcher, glove slightly above knee, upper body not leaning back). On the count of 3, pitcher strides forward and releases the ball. This drill makes pitchers gather their energy at the balance position so that the body and arm can come forward together toward home plate.

6.12 Toe Tap Drill (1-2-3 Drill)

Age Appropriate

Grouping 5, ages 10 to 15+

Objective

To develop an understanding of the importance of staying back, using a soft landing, and not rushing the delivery

Setup

Pitcher, catcher, pitching mound (optional), a baseball

Execution

Pitcher throws from a mound (or not) to a catcher at a shortened distance. Lifts leg and puts it down (counts 1), lifts leg and puts it down again (counts 2), lifts leg and throws on a count of 3. This drill teaches balance and coordination and builds strength in the back leg. The pitcher stays under control and avoids landing too hard, which can make throwing strikes difficult. Shoulders should stay fairly level without changing planes abruptly when the foot finally lands.

Pitcher Covering First Base Drill

6.13

Age Appropriate

Grouping 5, ages 10 to 15+

Objective

To get pitchers in the habit of covering first on balls hit to the right side and to work on the mechanics and communication involved with this play

Setup

Baseball field, pitching mound (optional), baseballs, pitchers, coach to hit or roll ground balls, catcher, first basemen, second baseman (optional)

Execution

Pitchers line up behind the mound with first basemen lined up at first. First pitcher throws a pitch from the mound to the catcher. Coach is at home plate with a fungo bat and a ball. After the ball crosses the plate, the coach hits or rolls a ball to the first baseman. Pitcher runs hard to a point near the baseline about 10 to 12 feet from the bag, then turns and runs parallel to the line, holding the glove at chest level as a target. First baseman flips to the pitcher as he runs down the line and before he gets to the bag. The ball should be tossed with an underhand flip as early as possible so the pitcher can catch the ball first and then find the bag. Pitcher should stop at the bag and make the play like a first baseman if the first baseman fails to field the ball cleanly. Coach can mix things up and hit comebackers to pitchers to keep them honest. Second basemen can be involved as well to work on communication between them and first basemen.

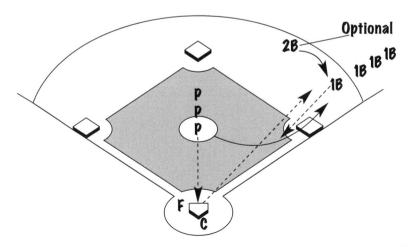

(continued)

6.13 Pitcher Covering First Base Drill
(continued)

 Coaching Keys

Young pitchers tend to jog all the way through this drill and take a path directly toward first base. Use cones to illustrate the proper path, if necessary. Make sure the pitcher sprints to the first cone, then gets under control and runs parallel to the baseline, presenting a target for the first baseman.

Comebacker Drill

6.14

Age Appropriate

Grouping 5, ages 10 to 15+

Objective

To allow pitchers to develop a feel for following through in fielding position, catching ground balls, moving feet toward first base, and making an accurate throw

Setup

Baseball field, pitching mound (optional), baseballs, pitchers, coach to hit or roll balls, catcher, first basemen

Execution

Pitchers line up behind the mound with first basemen lined up at first. The first pitcher throws a pitch from the mound to the catcher. Coach is at home plate with a fungo bat and a ball. After the ball crosses the plate, the coach hits or rolls a ball back to the pitcher, who fields it, steps toward the target, and follows the throw (not as exaggerated as an infielder). Also use this drill to practice double plays started by the pitcher.

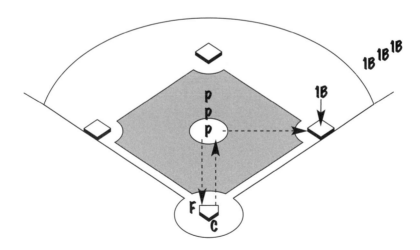

6.15 Bunt Drill

Age Appropriate

Grouping 5, ages 10 to 15+

Objective

To teach pitchers the mechanics of fielding bunts to various locations

Setup

Baseball field, pitching mound (optional), baseballs, pitchers, first basemen, coach to roll balls, catcher

Execution

Pitchers line up behind the mound with the first basemen lined up at first. First pitcher throws a pitch from the mound to the catcher. Coach is at home plate with a ball. After the pitch crosses the plate, the coach rolls a ball to simulate a bunt. Pitcher fields the bunt properly, generates momentum toward the target, and follows the throw. Stress footwork. On bunts to the first-base side, a right-hander opens up to first base before fielding the ball, generating momentum toward the target and throwing. A left-hander places the left foot between the ball and foul line and slowly turns the body to the glove side before fielding and making the throw (don't open too far; point the shoulder and generate momentum toward the target). Reverse the footwork on bunts to the third-base side. Add batters to make the bunts more realistic and to allow players to practice bunting. This drill can be combined with bunting drills by placing cones on the infield to illustrate where bunts should be placed.

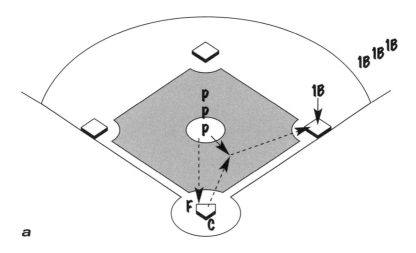

a

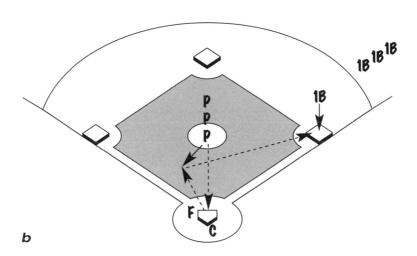

b

7

Fielding Drills

As soon as a pitch is delivered, it's time to play defense. The catcher must catch or block the pitch and sometimes must make a throw to a base to stop a runner who is stealing or attempting to advance on an errant pitch or passed ball. Sometimes the ball doesn't make it to the catcher, however. In those instances, the batter puts the ball in play, and someone on the defensive team must catch it and then make a throw to either record an out or keep the baserunners from advancing. If you can't catch the ball, there's really no need to throw it. But once you catch it, if you can't throw it, then what's the point of catching it at all (unless you're catching the third out of an inning)? So, to beat a dead horse, we'll say once more: Defense consists of catching and throwing—the ability to do one and not the other has little value. In this chapter we present drills to help players learn how to catch balls that are put into play. You'll also find drills that connect the throwing and catching fundamentals.

Keep in mind that outfielders and infielders of all ages and levels of play should catch batted balls the same way as the big league players do it. That is to say, the fundamentals employed should be identical. For this reason, big league players will work on many of the same simple drills you see here over and over every day before their games. Young players need to repeat the simple fundamental fielding drills in this book until they are so comfortable with the basic fundamentals that their bodies react naturally in game situations. Once the fundamental plays become second nature, you'll see your players start to make more acrobatic and complicated defensive plays. Kids need repetition after repetition, but they have limited attention spans; this means coaches must find ways to keep drills entertaining enough that players will continue to fine-tune their fundamentals without even knowing it. Always keep in mind that the teams that play catch the best generally win.

Outfield Drills

An outfielder's main job is to keep baserunners from taking extra bases. If a ball is hit in the air, it's the outfielder's duty to run down the ball and catch it, keeping the hitter off first base and, ideally, preventing other baserunners from advancing. If the ball is a sure base hit, the outfielder's responsibility is to get to the ball as quickly as possible, field it cleanly, and make an accurate throw to the proper cutoff or relay person. The goal is to keep a batter who has hit a routine single from going to second and to keep other runners from advancing farther than they should. If the ball is misplayed or thrown to the wrong base, runners can take extra bases. There is a direct correlation between these types of giveaways, runs allowed, and ultimately, winning and losing. Finally, when a ball is hit to someone else, it's the outfielder's job to back up the player who fielded the ball or the base to where the ball is being thrown so that if an errant throw is made, someone is there to keep the baserunners from advancing.

As you can see, the outfielder's job description is simple and straightforward. But that doesn't mean that playing outfield is easy. If it were, we wouldn't have an entire section of drills dedicated to outfield play. The drills in this section help players develop all the skills they need to become good outfielders. Sometimes in youth baseball the weaker players are put in the outfield, and their development is neglected. This type of thinking can limit the overall development of players and prove detrimental to a team's success.

Fielding Fly Balls

K E Y   P O I N T S

1. Get to the spot where the ball will land quickly; do not drift.

2. Watch the ball into the glove and catch the ball above the head using two hands whenever possible.

3. Try to move forward slightly as the catch is made.

7.1 Lite Flite Elimination

Age Appropriate

Grouping 1, all ages

Objective

To develop the proper technique for catching fly balls in a fun, competitive setting

Setup

Soft or sponge rubber balls, pitching machine (optional), coach to throw fly balls or to feed machine

Execution

Use soft or sponge rubber balls. Each player is thrown a fly ball (or fed a fly ball through a pitching machine). Younger players can use their gloves. Balls are so light that players have to catch the ball with two hands over the head. Older players and more advanced younger players can use bare hands. If players catch the ball, they stay in, but if they miss, they're out of the drill. This competition can also be done using the pass-pattern drill that follows or with real baseballs (when appropriate). When not using gloves, players should attempt to catch the ball with the glove hand only over the head. This makes them focus on proper hand positioning and watching the ball into the hand.

 Coaching Keys

Players who miss fly balls regularly usually aren't using proper technique and are likely taking their eyes off the ball. Make sure they catch the ball above their heads so that they can watch the ball travel all the way into the glove or hand.

7.2 Pass Patterns

Age Appropriate

Grouping 1, all ages

Objective

To develop proper crossover steps and drop steps and learn to catch fly balls on the run

Setup

A bucket of balls, a coach to throw "passes"

Execution

A coach or player (this can be long toss for pitchers) serves as quarterback. The fielding player tosses the ball to the quarterback and then uses a crossover or drop step in the appropriate direction before running a "pass pattern." The quarterback throws the ball high enough for the "receiver" to run under the ball and make a one-handed, over-the-shoulder catch. Have the player start over if the initial step is not executed correctly.

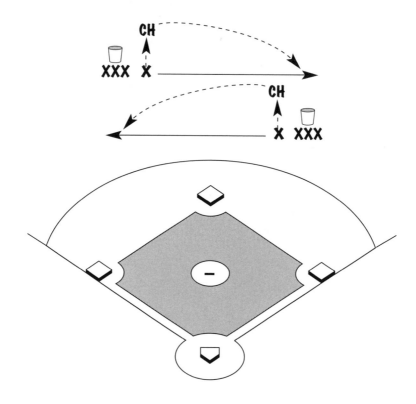

a

b

(continued)

125

Coaching Keys

The crossover step is the most efficient method of moving laterally on a baseball field. The crossover should be used by baserunners, infielders, and outfielders. To execute the step, a player pivots the foot nearest to where the ball is traveling while at the same time crossing the other foot over the first foot in the direction of the ball. If players are picking up the foot nearest the ball first and then crossing over, stop them immediately without throwing the pass and start over.

The drop step is a combination of a step back toward a ball hit over a player's head followed by a crossover in the direction of the ball. Again, stop the drill immediately and begin again if a player does not execute the initial step properly.

Thrown Fly Balls

7.3

Age Appropriate
Grouping 1, all ages

Objective
To learn to catch fly balls with two hands above the head in a controlled environment

Setup
A bucket of balls and a coach to throw balls to players; soft or sponge rubber balls for younger players

Execution
To prevent injury and embarrassment, players must be comfortable catching fly balls properly before fly balls are hit to them. The proper way to catch a fly ball is with two hands above the head so that eyes can follow the ball into the glove. The simplest way to teach proper execution is to throw fly balls to players and force them to do it correctly. Start with short, easy tosses and then adjust the height of throws to the skill and comfort level of players. You can start younger players out with soft baseballs or sponge rubber balls to avoid injury and build confidence. You can turn this drill into an elimination contest for the youngest players. Stress getting to the spot where the ball is coming down and catching with two hands above the head.

 Coaching Keys

Players who regularly miss fly balls are most likely not watching the ball and should perform the drill again and again, attempting to catch the ball with two hands above the head so that they can see the ball travel all the way into the glove. Many players catch fly balls while backpedaling or moving away from the infield. Try to get them to learn to catch the ball while moving slightly forward when executing this drill.

(continued)

Thrown or Machine Ground Balls 7.4

Age Appropriate
Grouping 1, all ages

Objective
To learn how to field ground balls properly in a controlled environment

Setup
A bucket of balls, a pitching machine (optional), a coach to feed machine or throw balls

Execution
Like infielders, outfielders should field a ground ball with a wide base, the butt down, and the hands out in front of the body. Get wide by stepping toward home with glove-side leg forward and glove in front of that foot. Players should get comfortable with proper fundamentals before fielding hit balls. It's okay to use a pitching machine for outfield ground balls right from the start. Roll or feed players ground balls one at a time. Have them get to the spot quickly, get under control, field properly, generate momentum toward the coach, and throw. Don't allow players to walk or run through ground balls. They need to slow down and get under control to field properly.

 Coaching Keys

Young outfielders have a tendency to "run through" ground balls. That is, they try to get to the spot quickly and then try to field the ball while still running at or near full speed. Remember that their main goal is to field the ball quickly and throw it to the proper cutoff or relay person to prevent baserunners from advancing. Thus, fielding the ball cleanly is the most important responsibility. Players should come to almost a complete stop if they have to so that they can be sure to field the ball cleanly.

(continued)

Communication Drill

7.5

Age Appropriate

Grouping 4, ages 7 to 15+

Objective

To understand the importance and mechanics of proper communication in the outfield

Setup

A bucket of baseballs, a coach to throw fly balls, soft or sponge rubber balls for younger players (optional), pitching machines (optional), a player to serve as a cutoff for throws (optional)

Execution

Outfielders form two lines at least 20 feet apart. The first players in each line step forward. The coach throws fly balls in between the two fielders, who must communicate and make the play. The player fielding the ball yells, "I got it!" at least three times. The other player then backs up the other player. The player who catches the ball should deliver a strong, accurate throw to the coach or cutoff player (a player who rotates out of the drill). For younger players, use soft baseballs, sponge rubber balls, or tennis balls. Use pitching machines to throw higher fly balls to more advanced players, ensuring the ball will reach about the same height and distance each time.

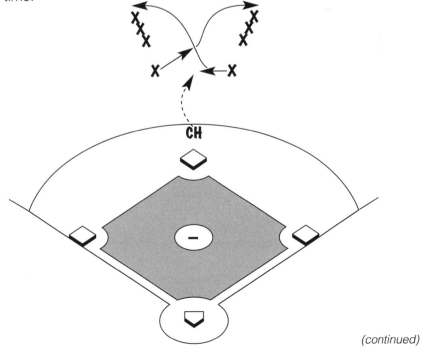

(continued)

7.5 Communication Drill *(continued)*

 Coaching Keys

The age-old outfield communication problem arises when two players call for the ball at the same time. Teach players that if there's any uncertainty as to who will make the catch, they should continue to call for the ball. If two players call for the ball at the same time and then one continues to call for it, that player should make the play. As players get older, this drill can be done by designating one player as the centerfielder, who has priority over any ball that he or she calls. In this format a third player can be added to simulate a game situation in which there are three outfielders. Again, the centerfielder is the quarterback and should call for any ball that he or she can easily get to.

Crossover Step Drill

7.6

Age Appropriate
Grouping 4, ages 7 to 15+

Objective
To develop a fundamentally sound crossover step

Setup
A bucket of balls and a coach to throw them

Execution
The crossover step (pivot one foot while crossing the other one over in the direction of the ball or the next base) is the most efficient way to move laterally on the baseball field. The crossover is an important technique for all fielders and baserunners. Outfielders line up, each with a ball. The first outfielder steps forward, tosses the ball to the coach, and assumes a ready position. The coach tells the player which way to go ahead of time. The player crosses over in that direction, then the coach tosses ball so it can be caught with two hands over the head. The player should concentrate on crossing over correctly until comfortable doing so. The coach should tell players which direction they'll be going ahead of time until they master the step. Then mix it up at will.

 Coaching Keys

As with Pass Patterns (page 124), stop this drill and start over if the player performs the crossover step incorrectly. The goal of this drill is to force the player to get to the spot quickly and catch the ball with two hands over the head. More difficult over-the-shoulder catches are practiced using the Pass Pattern Drill.

(continued)

a

b

Drop Step Drill

7.7

Age Appropriate

Grouping 5, ages 10 to 15+

Objective

To develop a fundamentally sound drop step

Setup

A bucket of balls and a coach to throw them

Execution

This drill is much like the drill for the crossover step but a bit more advanced. Players line up. The first player steps forward, tosses the ball to the coach, and assumes ready position. The coach says "Go!" and the player performs a drop step (drop one foot back, turn body, and cross the other foot over in the direction of the ball). The coach throws the ball directly over the player's head, high and close enough that he or she can catch it with two hands above the head.

 Coaching Keys

Have players take time to get footwork correct before tossing. As with Pass Patterns (page 124), stop this drill and start over if players do the drop step incorrectly. The goal of this drill is to force the player to get to the spot quickly and catch the ball with two hands over the head. More difficult over-the-shoulder catches are practiced using Pass Patterns.

(continued)

Drop Step Drill *(continued)*

a

b

c

Machine Fly Balls

7.8

Age Appropriate
Grouping 5, ages 10 to 15+

Objective
To allow players to work on catching more difficult fly balls

Setup
A bucket of balls, a pitching machine, a coach to feed the machine

Execution
A pitching machine can be a great asset to coaches who aren't comfortable hitting fly balls. Pitching machines can throw fly balls virtually as high as you want and to almost the same spot every time. Just be sure that your players are confident enough and capable enough to catch these balls. If you're unsure, use soft balls or tennis balls instead of baseballs. Don't ruin a player's confidence or create a potential injury situation because you want to make your practices more exciting.

 Coaching Keys

In general, fly balls fed through a machine have a slightly different spin on them than do batted balls. The spin causes the balls to fall almost straight down to the ground once they reach their highest point. This can be tricky for young outfielders who are accustomed to trying to move back to the spot where the ball is going to land, so it's important that players have developed their skills enough to be able to perform this drill safely. One benefit of catching fly balls fed through a pitching machine is that players are usually forced to learn to catch the ball while moving forward, which is not an easy skill to teach or master.

7.9 Fence Drill

Age Appropriate

Grouping 5, ages 10 to 15+

Objective

To learn the importance of field awareness and how to pursue fly balls hit near the outfield fence

Setup

A bucket of balls and a coach to throw them

Execution

This drill teaches outfielders to be aware of their surroundings. The activity is not intended to practice robbing home runs, but that element can be added for fun. Each player gets in line with a ball. The first player tosses the ball to the coach, who throws a fly ball that will land on the warning track. The player races back, feels for the fence with his or her bare hand, and then catches the ball with two hands over the head.

 Coaching Keys

Young players often miss fly balls because they take their eyes off the ball to find the fence. They should first glance back to where they are running and then pick up the ball without looking at the fence again. Once they get to the warning track, have them start feeling for the fence with their throwing hand. At this point they should remain focused on the flight of the ball.

Hitting Balls to Outfielders

7.10

Age Appropriate

Grouping 5, ages 10 to 15+

Objective

To give outfielders a more realistic look at balls coming off a bat

Setup

A bucket of balls, a fungo bat (or any bat), a coach to hit, a player or coach to catch throws

Execution

Just as is true for infielders, it's important to hit balls of all kinds to your outfielders. Most of the drills and skills mentioned here for outfielders can be performed with coaches hitting balls. Again, it's important that the coach understands the skill level of the players he is hitting to and to adapt accordingly, sometimes even from one player to the next. Don't hit balls too high or too hard or use hard baseballs until players are confident catching ground balls and fly balls the right way. Once they're comfortable, repetitions are the best way for outfielders to improve.

Infield Drills

Baseball is a game of repetition, and that's most evident in the infield. Although you'll see all kinds of gimmicks and gadgets designed to help infielders develop soft hands and improve their eye–hand coordination, the bottom line is that you're allowed to use a glove to play defense, so why not learn to use it properly?

Big league infielders take ground balls every day in spring training, in practice, and before games. And they do it the same way every time, with a wide base, the butt down, and the hands out in front. They work on routine ground balls, backhands, and forehands. They throw the ball to first base and practice starting and turning double plays. They do the same basic drills every single day for at least eight months out of the year. Then many of them do it all over again during the off-season to stay sharp.

There's a reason that big league infielders focus on the same skills and drills that we discuss in this section. When a ball is hit to an infielder in a game situation, everything happens quickly. The batter is sprinting to first, and other runners are heading toward other bases. The infielder must process a great deal of information very quickly just to determine where to throw the ball; if he or she must also spend time thinking about how to field the ball properly and how the ball should be thrown, chances are that everyone is going to be safe. Fielding, throwing, and catching must become second nature for infielders, and to reach that point they have to work constantly on developing their fundamental skills. In this section we'll give you all the basics you need to make your team's infield defense stronger.

Fielding Ground Balls

K E Y   P O I N T S

1. Create a wide base with the feet.

2. Butt stays down; don't bend only at the waist.

3. Hands are out in front; see the ball into the glove.

4. Relax wrists; fingers point down and barely touch the ground.

7.11 Rolled Ground Balls

Age Appropriate
Grouping 1, all ages

Objective
To help infielders become comfortable with the proper mechanics of fielding a ground ball

Setup
A bucket of balls and a coach to roll them

Execution
This drill is simple and appropriate for all ages. Balls can be rolled as soft or as hard as necessary; the type of hop the ball takes can be controlled. Players assume the ground ball position with a wide base, butt down, and hands out in front (the glove-hand wrist is relaxed so the coach can see inside the glove and the fingers are pointing down). Use a flat surface to prevent bad hops, and bad habits. At first, the ball should be rolled directly into a player's glove from about 10 feet away. Have players hold the ground ball position for five reps so that they can feel a little burn in their thighs. As players get comfortable fielding ground balls properly, the coach can move back and roll balls harder. For conditioning, older players can be asked to hold the position for more reps. The ball must be caught out in front so that the eyes can follow the ball into the glove.

Coaching Keys

If the ball doesn't stay in a player's glove or if the player seems to be getting handcuffed quite a bit by bad hops, check the player's glove positioning and angle. The glove should be out in front of the body with the wrist relaxed to the point that the fingers of the glove are pointing almost straight down. If a player is having trouble getting the glove into the proper position, have him or her reach back between the legs and scrape dirt forward with the glove until it's in the proper position in front of the body. If the glove is out in front and the wrist is relaxed, a player is more likely to see the bad hop early and move the glove to a position in which the ball can still be caught.

7.12 Throwing After the Catch Drill

Age Appropriate
Grouping 1, all ages

Objective
To understand and apply the concept of using the body's momentum to make a stronger throw

Setup
A bucket of balls, a coach or player to receive throws, a coach or player to roll ground balls (optional), a target (optional), three cones or markers

Execution
This drill reinforces the concept of catching the ground ball first, generating momentum toward the target, throwing the ball, and following the throw. Set up three cones several feet apart, placed in a line toward the target to where the throw will be made (easiest to set up as a simulation of the 5-4 force out at second base). Cones should be placed so that the distance is appropriate to accomplish the intended result for the age group involved. A player sets up with the right foot next to first cone and assumes the ground ball fielding position (wide base, butt down, hands in front). A ball is rolled by the coach to the player, who fields it, or the player starts with a ball and simulates the fielding position. The player shuffles the feet to the second cone, releases the ball, and follows the throw past the third cone and toward the target. Emphasize the four-seam grip. Ball can be thrown to a coach or another teammate. The player should stay low and not stand straight up after fielding the ball. This drill can be turned into a contest by placing a chest- or head-high target at second base with a net or screen behind to catch errant throws. Players who hit the target stay alive, and those who miss are eliminated. If there's nobody to roll the balls, players can get a ball out of the bucket, assume the ground ball fielding position, and then execute the drill.

 Coaching Keys

Players who aren't throwing the ball accurately are likely dropping the elbow below the shoulder or are peeling off away from the target before following the throw all the way past the third cone. For players making the latter mistake, set up another cone about five feet to the left of the third cone and make them follow the throw all the way through the last two cones before peeling off.

7.12

Players who are throwing the ball high or low are likely standing up before shuffling and throwing. Remember: Stay low and go low. The first movement upon catching the ball is toward the target. Players should shuffle in that direction, keeping the knees bent in an athletic position instead of standing straight up. This keeps the head, shoulders, and eyes level, which makes it easier to stay focused on the target.

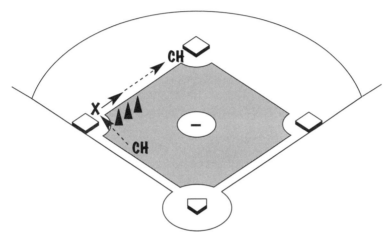

7.13 Throwing-Side Foot Backhand Drill

Age Appropriate

Grouping 4, ages 7 to 15+

Objective

To learn and practice proper technique for backhanding ground balls to the throwing-hand side

Setup

A bucket of balls, a coach to roll balls, cones or markers (optional)

Execution

This backhand is used for hard-hit balls slightly to the player's backhand side. Just like a regular ground ball, the backhand is caught out in front of the body so the eyes can follow the ball into the glove and the wrist and forearm don't get in the way. Players also need to establish a wide base with the butt down. A player lines up in front of a coach with the right leg extended. Player pivots the right foot so the instep faces the coach and drops the left knee to the ground (opposite for lefties). This creates a wide base to help get the butt down, and the glove is placed in front of the right foot and toward the coach. Coach should be close enough to roll balls directly into the glove until the player gets the hang of catching the ball out in front with one hand, squeezing the glove, and bringing it to the center of the body. Ball is rolled directly toward the front foot. Glove-hand wrist should be relaxed so the coach can see into glove. Tell players to avoid twisting the glove so they don't close it too soon. After five repetitions, have another player try. As players get more advanced they can raise the trail knee off the ground a few inches. Adding repetitions can help with conditioning.

7.14 Glove-Side Foot Backhand Drill

Age Appropriate

Grouping 4, ages 7 to 15+

Objective

To learn and practice proper technique for backhanding ground balls to the glove-hand side

Setup

A bucket of balls, a coach to roll balls, cones or markers (optional)

Execution

This backhand provides more reach for players ranging farther to their backhand side. Just as for a regular ground ball, the backhand is caught out in front of the body so the eyes can follow the ball into the glove and the wrist and forearm don't get in the way. Players need to establish a wide base with the butt down. A player lines up in front of a coach and crosses the glove-side leg over the other leg as if turning to walk. The throwing-side knee is dropped to the ground, much like a walking lunge. Player creates a wide base to help get the butt down and the glove in front of the body. Ball is caught off the front foot instead of in front of it (but still out in front of the body). Coach should be close enough to roll balls directly into glove until player gets the hang of catching the ball out in front with one hand, squeezing the glove, and bringing it to the center of the body. Ball is rolled slightly in front of the lead foot. Glove-hand wrist should be relaxed so coach can see into the glove. Tell players to avoid twisting the glove so they don't close it too soon. After five repetitions, have another player try. As players get more advanced they can raise the trail knee off the ground a few inches. Adding repetitions can help with conditioning.

 Coaching Keys

For all backhands, the most common mistake is the ball jumping up and smacking off the player's wrist instead of going into the glove. This happens when the glove is positioned behind the player's body, which creates a glove angle in which the wrist is actually forward of the glove. By placing the glove in front of the body, the wrist is naturally relaxed in such a manner that it doesn't get in the way if a ball takes a tricky hop. Again, just as with the technique for fielding a basic ground ball, the fingers of the glove should point straight down toward the ground.

7.14

An error frequently made when it comes to backhands is twisting the glove. This may happen because young players have gloves that aren't fully broken in or don't feel that they're strong enough to just squeeze the ball and keep it in the glove. The problem is that sometimes they start to twist the glove before the ball gets there, preventing the ball from entering the glove. Players should squeeze the ball when it enters the glove and bring it straight to their chest for the transfer and throw.

7.15 High Five Drill (Underhand Flip)

Age Appropriate

Grouping 4, ages 7 to 15+

Objective

To understand and apply the concept of generating momentum toward the target when executing an underhand flip and to develop the habit of leaving the hand at face level after the flip

Setup

A bucket of balls, a coach to roll balls, cones or markers (optional)

Execution

The underhand flip is used by virtually all infielders at some point, so it should be introduced at a young age and practiced. Players line up opposite the coach, 10 to 15 feet away. One at a time, players assume basic ground ball position (wide base, butt down, hands in front). The coach rolls balls to the first player. The player catches the ball first, generates momentum toward target, uses an underhand flip, and finishes by following the flip toward the coach with the hand held high at head level. When the player gets to the coach, he gives the coach a high five (hand should not drop below head level until high five is completed). Player uses body momentum to carry the toss to the target. Wrist remains stiff. Avoid letting the ball roll off the fingers.

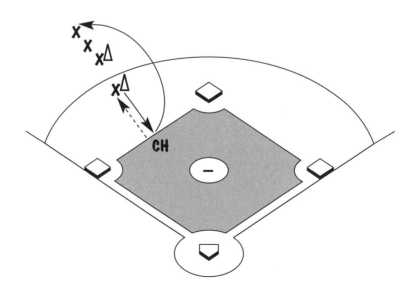

 Coaching Keys

This drill reminds players to keep the hand held high after the flip. Failure to keep the hand high is one of the most common mistakes when it comes to executing the underhand flip. Generally, wherever the hand ends up is the direction in which the ball is going to travel, and it's easier for the person receiving the flip to catch the ball if it's at chest or head level.

7.16 Box Drill (Underhand Flip), Short to Second

Age Appropriate

Grouping 4, ages 7 to 15+

Objective

To simulate and practice the underhand flip from shortstop to second base

Setup

At least five players forming a box (two players on one corner), baseballs, cones or markers (optional)

Execution

Create a box with four players standing up to 25 feet apart (closer for younger players). A fifth player stands behind a player at any corner. The first toss originates from the corner where there are two players. Players don't use gloves (playing with bare hands increases concentration). Each player faces the corner to his or her right. The tosser shuffles his or her feet or crosses over, flips the ball to the player at the corner to his or her left, leaves the hand high, and follows the flip to that corner. After arriving at the next corner, he or she turns to face the corner to the right, holding two hands out in front, ready to receive the toss as the ball comes around. The player catches the ball first, generates momentum, tosses, and follows to the next corner. Stress maintaining a stiff wrist, no extra arm motion, leaving the hand high, and following the flip. This drill can be done with players of any age. For younger players, use gloves or softer balls. Count to see which group of five can catch the most in a row without missing one.

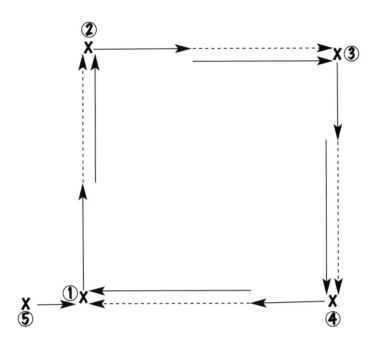

7.17 Box Drill (Underhand Flip), Second to Short

Age Appropriate

Grouping 4, ages 7 to 15+

Objective

To simulate and practice the underhand flip from second base to short-stop

Setup

At least five players forming a box (two players on one corner), baseballs, cones or markers (optional)

Execution

Create a box with four players standing up to 25 feet apart (closer for younger players). A fifth player stands behind a player at any one of the corners. The first toss originates from the corner where there are two play-ers. Don't use gloves (playing with bare hands increases concentration). Each player faces the corner to his or her left. The tosser shuffles feet or crosses over, keeps the hand with the ball in front of the body, flips the ball to player at the corner to the right without turning the body, leaves the hand high, and follows the flip to that corner. After arriving at the next corner, he or she turns to face the corner to the left, holding two hands out in front, ready to receive the toss as the ball comes around. He or she catches the ball first, generates momentum, flips, and follows to the next corner. This technique is awkward because the hand stays in front of the body at all times. It's important to keep the wrist stiff and avoid turning the body completely toward target so that the hand is no longer in front. For younger players, use gloves or softer balls. Count to see which group of five can catch the most in a row without missing one.

 Coaching Keys

Players might tend to turn and bring their hand behind their leg to execute this flip. This takes extra time and makes it harder for the shortstop to pick up where the toss is coming from. To avoid this, remind players that they're catching the ball out in front of their body, so that's the point from which the flip should be made.

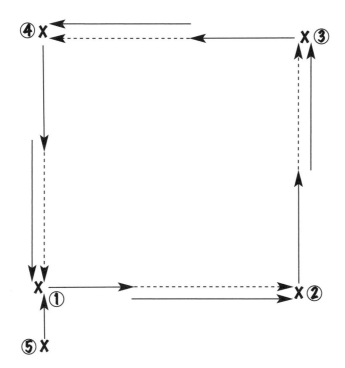

7.18 4-6/6-4 Drill

Age Appropriate

Grouping 4, ages 7 to 15+

Objective

To practice getting force outs at second base using the underhand flip

Setup

A bucket of balls, a coach to roll balls, cones or markers, first basemen (optional)

Execution

This drill allows players to work on putting the double play together. One group lines up at shortstop. Another group lines up at second. The coach rolls a ground ball to the first player in the shortstop line. The first player in the second-base line runs to the bag, puts his or her left foot on the bag, and holds up both hands at chest level as a target. The shortstop fields the ball and executes an underhand flip to the second baseman, who takes his or her right foot to the ball and catches it. The second baseman returns the ball to the coach, and players go to the end of opposite lines. After each player has several turns, switch and work on the 4-6 double-play feed, in which the drill is reversed. The difference here is that the shortstop puts his or her right foot on bag and takes the left foot toward the ball. As players get comfortable, they can throw to a coach or teammates at first base to complete the double play. Stress the underhand flip and that players covering second base must get there fast enough to be stationary targets for their teammates.

 Coaching Keys

Typically, the most common problem with this drill also frequently happens in game situations: The player covering the base doesn't get there quickly enough to be a stationary target. This means the player fielding the ball must throw to a moving target, which compromises accuracy, and the player covering must catch the ball on the move like a wide receiver going over the middle. Stress that the player covering the base should break as soon as the ball is rolled to the fielder so that he or she can be a stationary target.

Another problem that can arise with this drill is the location from which the ball is rolled. The ball should be rolled from a position that simulates how the ball would travel off the bat from home plate. If you stand in front of the fielder and roll the ball, the mechanics of the flip are different than they would be if the ball were coming off the bat because the fielder's shoulders are not square to home plate. The coach rolling the balls should align in a straight line between home plate and the shortstop or second baseman to better simulate the direction that a ball travels in a game.

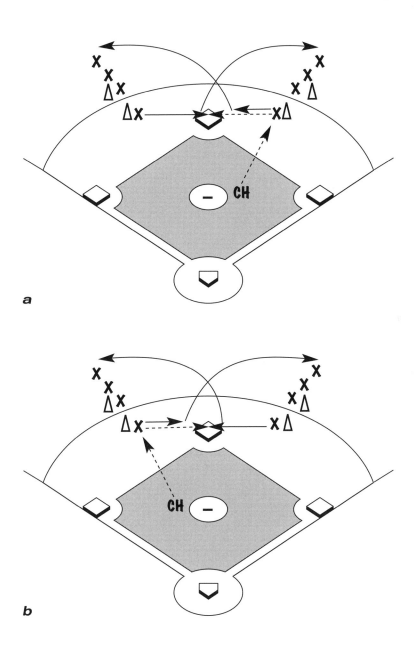

a

b

7.19 First Base Drill

Age Appropriate

Grouping 4, ages 7 to 15+

Objective

To develop proper mechanics when receiving throws at first base

Setup

A bucket of balls, a player or coach to throw, first basemen, an empty bucket

Execution

Players line up in foul territory near first base. The coach sets up anywhere in the infield with a bucket of balls. An empty bucket is placed near first base. The first player comes to first base and puts the heel of the throwing-side foot on the base. The coach throws the ball to this player. The player sees the ball coming across the diamond and takes his or her glove and glove-side foot directly toward the ball together. The ball should hit the glove at the same time the foot lands. This prevents stretching too soon. Stress that first basemen get to the bag quickly, stand tall, square shoulders to the infielder making the throw, and take the glove and glove-side foot toward the ball together. Remind them not to stretch prematurely. You can also have players work on receiving errant throws and short hops.

 Coaching Keys

If players are stretching too soon, make them exaggerate the step with the glove foot so that the foot lands on the ground at the exact same time the ball enters the glove.

Backhand Throwing Drill

7.20

Age Appropriate

Grouping 5, ages 10 to 15+

Objective

To practice generating momentum back toward the target after back-handing ground balls

Setup

A bucket of balls, a coach or player to roll balls, cones or markers, a player or coach to receive throws

Execution

This drill is very similar to a regular throwing drill. Two cones are set up. A player sets up in ready position to the right of the first cone. The coach rolls a ball to the player's backhand. The player fields the ball using either backhand method, stops his or her momentum, shuffles back to the first cone, throws, and follows the throw past the second cone. This player then goes to the end of the line. Stopping momentum going away from the target and then shuffling back toward the target is a difficult concept for young players to understand and should be stressed. No off-balance throws.

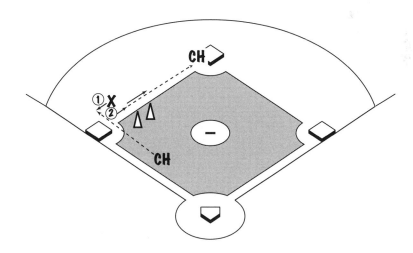

7.21 Machine Backhands and Forehands

Age Appropriate
Grouping 5, ages 10 to 15+

Objective
To work on getting to a spot quickly and catching the ball in front of the body on backhands and forehands

Setup
A bucket of balls, a pitching machine aimed to the same spot, cones or markers

Execution
Set up a cone in one spot; position a pitching machine to roll hard ground balls straight at the cone. Have players line up to the right or left of the cone so if they break when the ball is fed, they'll have to backhand or forehand the ball without getting in front of it. Players should break as the ball is fed through the machine, focusing on catching the ball out in front of their body at the cone. Alternate from one side to the other so players get both backhands and forehands. This drill can easily be turned into an elimination contest. Players should switch lines after catching a ground ball.

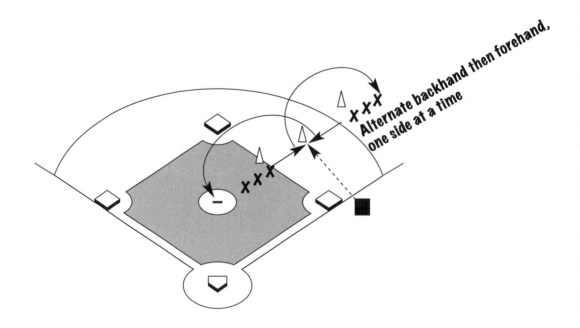

Alternate backhand then forehand, one side at a time

Coaching Keys

If players struggle to field balls cleanly because they're still on the move, allow them to break before the ball is fed and to set up in the backhand position before the ball arrives. Once they get comfortable making the play correctly with their gloves out in front of their bodies, have them break as the ball is fed to make the play more difficult.

7.22 Machine Short Hops

Age Appropriate

Grouping 5, ages 10 to 15+

Objective

To develop soft hands and a proper glove angle; to work on catching the ball out in front of the body

Setup

A bucket of balls (soft or sponge balls or real baseballs) and a pitching machine

Execution

This drill can be done outdoors or indoors. You can make the drill even more challenging by having players field soft or sponge rubber balls with their bare hands. Set pitching machines so that players must field fast-moving balls on short hops. Make sure players assume and maintain a good fielding position (wide base, butt down, hands out in front). If using gloves and real baseballs, they'll need to relax their wrists and catch the ball out in front. Have them try to catch the ball with only one hand to promote proper glove angle and softer hands. (This is especially important when using softer balls and no gloves.) See who can catch the most short hops out of 5 or 10 attempts.

 Coaching Keys

Players who have trouble fielding these balls cleanly are probably not getting their gloves or hands far enough out in front, and their wrists might not be relaxed. Have them assume the proper hand and wrist position before the balls are fed to force them to watch the ball travel all the way into their hands. The relaxed wrist makes their hands "softer" and allows them to field the balls more cleanly.

7.23 Hitting Ground Balls

Age Appropriate

Grouping 5, ages 10 to 15+

Objective

To get a more realistic sense of fielding ground balls coming off a bat

Setup

A bucket of baseballs, a fungo bat (or another type of bat), a coach to hit balls

Execution

At some point it becomes necessary to hit ground balls to your team. Before you do this—at any level—make sure you have introduced the players to the basic ground ball fundamentals and given them a chance to get comfortable fielding balls the proper way. Use common sense when hitting ground balls. If the field is not in good condition, take it easy. Adapt the speed of the balls to each player's skill level. Players getting beaten up with bad hops in practice are not getting better.

If you have more than one coach who can hit ground balls accurately, here's a way to maximize repetitions: One coach hits to the third basemen and shortstops from the first-base side while the other hits to second and first from the third-base side. After a few minutes, one coach goes "live," with the players fielding his or her balls throwing to first. The other players just lob the balls back to their coach on one hop or place the balls in a bucket. The first basemen take throws and stop fielding ground balls at this point. Each position gets to go "live" before the drill ends. As players get older, they can hit ground balls to each other if there aren't enough coaches. Having one person hit to each position is ideal but not always possible.

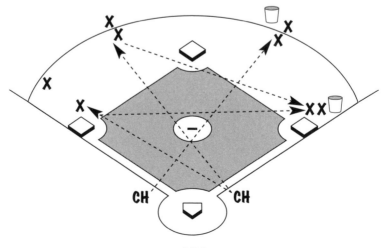

PART III

Practicing the Ripken Way

Practice Planner

One of the major goals of this book is to provide coaches with a format for running effective practices. When we say *effective,* we mean efficient and enjoyable. You want to make the best use of the limited time and space that you have and be able to maintain the interest of your players while helping them improve. To this point, we have presented ideas and philosophies to help you do this. In the following chapters, you'll find basic practice formats for the various age breakdowns that we've presented. But we don't want to tell you everything. We know that as coaches you'll want to develop your own new, fun, and creative ideas, and we encourage you to incorporate those into your practices.

In the following chapters, you'll find suggested practice formats for each age group. In some places, we make specific suggestions, and in others we give you the option of choosing from many different drills within a particular grouping. We advise you to mix things up and use different drills from the same groupings on different days to keep things more interesting for you and your players. Refer to the Practice Planner to find the drills that are appropriate for your team. The Practice Planner also helps you quickly locate the description of the drills you choose to use; in this way we hope to make planning your practices a little easier.

We know that there are drills out there that you or other coaches have found to be effective. You are encouraged to incorporate those drills into your practices and to pass them along to us by sending an e-mail via our *Coach's Clipboard* Web site at **www.ripkenbaseball. com/cc.** Address any correspondence to **newsletter@ripkenbase-ball.com.** We hope the way we've grouped our drills will help you determine where any additional drills you choose to use will fit into your practice plans.

Remember that there's no reason that practices can't be as much fun, or even more fun, for the kids as games are. Practice time is when players improve. Keep this in mind as you create your game schedules and are trying to decide which tournaments to enter. Kids love playing games and competing, but if you neglect practice, you'll never have an opportunity to help them work on the problem areas that surface during competition.

Grouping 1			All Ages
Drill title	**Drill number**	**Page number**	**Category**
Free Hitting	5.1	64	Fun hitting drill
Hitting Contests	5.3	66	Fun hitting drill
Tee Hitting for Distance	5.6	70	Fun hitting drill
Soft Toss	5.7	72	Regular hitting drill
Tee Work	5.8	74	Regular hitting drill
Short Toss From the Front	5.9	76	Regular hitting drill
Bunting Drill	5.11	80	Regular hitting drill
Baserunning Relays	5.14	86	Fun baserunning drill
Big League Baserunning	5.15	87	Fun baserunning drill
Head to Head	5.16	89	Fun baserunning drill
Cutoff Relay Race	6.1	94	Fun throwing drill
Twenty-One	6.5	100	Fun throwing drill
Other Throwing Games	6.6	101	Fun throwing drill
One-Knee Drill	6.7	105	Throwing/pitching drill
Power Position Drill	6.9	108	Throwing/pitching drill
Lite Flite Elimination	7.1	122	Fun outfield drill
Pass Patterns	7.2	124	Fun outfield drill
Thrown Fly Balls	7.3	127	Regular outfield drill
Thrown or Machine Ground Balls	7.4	129	Regular outfield drill
Rolled Ground Balls	7.11	142	Regular infield drill
Throwing After the Catch Drill	7.12	144	Regular infield drill
Grouping 2			**Ages 4 to 9**
Goalie Game	5.2	65	Fun hitting drill
Knock Out the Catcher	5.4	67	Fun hitting drill
Throw for Distance	6.4	99	Fun throwing drill
Grouping 3			**Ages 4 to 12**
Line Drive Home Run Derby	5.5	69	Fun hitting drill
Slip and Slide	5.17	90	Fun baserunning drill
Long-Toss Golf	6.2	96	Fun throwing drill
Shoot and Score!	6.3	98	Fun throwing drill

Grouping 4			Ages 7 to 15+
Drill title	**Drill number**	**Page number**	**Category**
Stickball Drill	5.10	78	Regular hitting drill
Tee Drill	6.8	107	Throwing/pitching drill
Long Toss	6.10	110	Throwing/pitching drill
Balance Position Drill	6.11	111	Pitching drill
Communication Drill	7.5	131	Regular outfield drill
Crossover Step Drill	7.6	133	Regular outfield drill
Throwing-Side Foot Backhand Drill	7.13	146	Regular infield drill
Glove-Side Foot Backhand Drill	7.14	148	Regular infield drill
High Five Drill (Underhand Flip)	7.15	150	Regular infield drill
Box Drill (Underhand Flip), Short to Second	7.16	152	Regular infield drill
Box Drill (Underhand Flip), Second to Short	7.17	154	Regular infield drill
4-6/6-4 Drill	7.18	156	Regular infield drill
First Base Drill	7.19	158	Regular infield drill
Grouping 5			Ages 10 to 15+
One-Arm Drill	5.12	82	Advanced hitting drill
Lob Toss	5.13	83	Advanced hitting drill
Toe Tap Drill (1-2-3 Drill)	6.12	112	Pitching drill
Pitcher Covering First Base Drill	6.13	113	Pitching drill
Comebacker Drill	6.14	115	Pitching drill
Bunt Drill	6.15	116	Pitching drill
Drop Step Drill	7.7	135	Advanced outfield drill
Machine Fly Balls	7.8	137	Advanced outfield drill
Fence Drill	7.9	138	Advanced outfield drill
Hitting Balls to Outfielders	7.10	139	Advanced outfield drill
Backhand Throwing Drill	7.20	159	Advanced infield drill
Machine Backhands and Forehands	7.21	160	Advanced infield drill
Machine Short Hops	7.22	162	Advanced infield drill
Hitting Ground Balls	7.23	164	Advanced infield drill

8

Practice Particulars for Ages 4 to 6

Nothing is more rewarding for a parent or coach than to see the joy and excitement on a young person's face when he or she arrives for baseball or T-ball practices or games. At the youngest ages, most of the kids have seen baseball on television or in person, have been curious enough to pick up a bat or glove, and genuinely are excited about the sport.

Parents who are athletically minded and want their kids to participate in sports are eager to take their children to practices and games. They hope their children will have the same positive athletic experiences they had as kids and will pursue sports as part of an active lifestyle that they can carry on throughout their lives and eventually pass on to their own children. The first day of baseball or T-ball practice, especially for those of the youngest ages, is usually full of smiles, laughter, and enthusiasm.

However, if we drop by to see the same group of kids at practice a month later, the scene often has changed dramatically. The kids with parents who are either crazy about baseball or who played the game and grew to love it generally are happy on the baseball field no matter what. They get a healthy dose of the game at home, have been taught some of the game's basic rules, and probably spend quality time with their parents watching games in person or on television. Because of the positive reinforcement they get about the game at home and their desire to please their parents, these children have fun playing and practicing the game.

But what happened to the other kids? Where have the smiles gone? Where's the bounce in their step? How come they seem to be more interested in rolling down the hill or chasing their teammates around the playground? Why aren't mom and dad as happy about bringing them to practices and games?

There is no great mystery to this. The kids are not having fun and would rather be doing other things, but the parents feel obligated to bring them anyway because they made a commitment and paid their league dues. Why does this happen?

It's easy to blame the coach. However, as we said earlier, many of the volunteer coaches, especially those at the youngest levels, are coaching out of the goodness of their hearts. Maybe no one else wanted to coach. Or maybe the coach's child has some behavior or attention issues, and the parent decided to coach so the child's experience and the experience of the other children would be enhanced. Whatever the reason, more times than not, this coach is a concerned parent more than a baseball coach. He or she might never have played the game beyond the youth league level—or maybe never at all.

Parents willing to volunteer their time, to squeeze baseball practices and games into busy work schedules and family lives, are the lifeblood of our sport at the grassroots level. Generally, as kids get older, the parents who care the most and who understand the game move to the forefront and become coaches. At the youngest levels, most people don't know what sport they want their kids to play. They want to try them all, to promote an active lifestyle, and to figure out what's best for their children. These parents just want to provide their kids with a positive experience. Whether their children take more of a liking to baseball or soccer or basketball really isn't important. Sports provide their children with a structured, active environment in which they can have fun with other kids.

The bottom line is that if a parent has a bad experience with baseball or T-ball when his or her child is 4 years old, that parent will look for another activity. In many cases, the child won't have a choice. So, if you add it all up—inexperienced volunteer coaches, kids who are just learning the game and have short attention spans, and critical parents—there's a pretty good chance that a lot of people are going to have less than positive initial baseball experiences.

For a child, the initial sports experience leaves a lasting impression. Certainly if soccer or basketball is a lot more exciting than baseball, mom and dad are going to hear about it or notice that their little one is excited to go to all of his or her practices except for baseball practice. A child's first couple of years on the field might determine whether he or she will fall in love with the sport and stick with it.

Because initial athletic experiences can make a huge impression on both parents and children, and if youth baseball coaches at the grassroots level are the lifeblood of the game of baseball, wouldn't it make sense to arm even the coaches of the youngest age groups with the information they need to make the experience as enjoyable as possible for everyone involved? We would argue that it might be *most* important to supply these coaches with information.

Teaching children between the ages of 4 and 6 can present challenges in terms of the players' emotional and physical maturity, attention spans, and motor-skill development that are not found among the older age groups. Because of these challenges, and because of the importance we place on providing the youngest players with a positive introduction to the sport, we'll present an in-depth philosophical look at how to construct a practice for this age group. We'll go into more detail than we will for other age groups. Repetition of fundamental skills in an attempt to promote the development of muscle memory, and providing a safe and thoroughly enjoyable experience are essential for players at this age.

As people who have benefited tremendously from the game of baseball and who care considerably about the game's future, we feel it's important to help the coaches who are so vital to the sport's growth. We're confident that if you follow the guidelines we lay out here, your baseball experience and that of your players will be positive. In the long run, everyone wins: coaches, players, parents, and the sport as a whole.

Harnessing the Energy

The first thing you'll notice when coaching a group of 4- to 6-year-olds is their energy level. Usually on the first day of practice they sprint from their cars to the field, bursting with enthusiasm. They immediately dive into the ball bag and start playing catch with dad or a friend. Or they might pick up a bat and start swinging. The atmosphere might be a bit chaotic, but it's heartwarming to see the smiles and the excitement in their eyes.

As a coach, this is your opportunity to make a great first impression on your team—and also to reinforce the positive impression you've already made during your first contact with your team's parents. We do hope at this point you've contacted parents via e-mail or telephone or held a group meeting with them to introduce yourself, explain your goals for the season, and answer any questions they might have. So, as we said, the parents should already be impressed by your organization and your eagerness to open the lines of communication. Now you just have to win over the kids—and usually that's not too difficult.

To begin, we recommend that you have the kids sit down on the grass or in the bench area although they are ready to run around and go crazy. Get to know them a little bit. Find out their names, their favorite teams and players, and what positions they like best. Making name tags for each player will help you learn their names quickly and show parents you really care and want to get to know their children.

You'll need to have a practice plan that you can move right into as soon as everyone arrives. There's nothing worse than down time and standing around when you're dealing with a group this young. If you haven't had anyone volunteer earlier, see if any parents are willing to help out with that particular practice. If so, be sure to take a few minutes to share with them exactly what you plan to do. Find out what skills they're comfortable working with and make assignments accordingly.

Working the Plan

When planning a practice for the youngest players, keep in mind the goal areas we established for the 4- to 6-year-old age group in chapter 3; these will be your priorities for the season:

1. Learning the basic rules—the right direction to run when the ball is hit; runners must touch the bases; how to record outs (catch the ball in the air, throw to first, or tag the runners); running past first base; scoring a run; three outs constitute an inning.

2. Throwing mechanics—turn the body so that the front shoulder points toward the target; keep the elbow above the shoulder; step toward the target with the nonthrowing foot and release the ball.

3. Tracking—follow the ball with the eyes into the glove, whether on the ground or in the air (use softer balls); use two hands to catch and field; try to catch the ball out in front of the body.

4. Hitting—how to hold and swing the bat; batting safety (when not to swing bats, wearing batting helmets); hitting off a tee; hitting softly tossed pitches.

5. Learning positional play—if the ball is hit to your buddy, let him or her field it (note to coach: try not to put more than 10 players on a field at a time).

Keep these goals in mind and incorporate them into as many practices as possible. We understand that in most cases your league is not going to provide you with much in the way of equipment. In most instances, teams are allotted three or four safety baseballs, three or four batting helmets, a batting tee, and two or three bats. This is not enough to run a very thorough practice. Keep in mind that for this age group a lot can be accomplished using tennis balls or another kind of soft rubber or foam ball. Fielding and catching are difficult motor skills to develop, but they become nearly impossible if kids are afraid of being hurt by the ball.

Young players can learn to track and catch by using a larger, softer ball.

Having plenty of balls on hand is important. If you don't mind spending a few dollars as a volunteer coach, we suggest investing in a bucket of soft sponge or rubber balls, or even safety baseballs (see Resources, page 233). There are really cool sponge balls out there with seams just like a real baseball—a great invention for kids of this age group. In fact, these balls are a nice product for older kids, too, especially when space is limited for off-season workouts and practices must be moved indoors because of weather. These balls are dense enough that they can be thrown accurately, and they fly a pretty good distance when they're hit. If you can't afford to purchase these balls, or would prefer not to, find an old five-gallon bucket and ask your local tennis club for some used tennis balls. Having plenty of balls on hand is an important part of running a smooth, efficient practice. When dealing with this age group we're most concerned about safety and developing mechanics and motor skills. Until kids have developed their catching skills, real baseballs can be thrown to coaches or at targets or nets, which greatly reduces the risk of injury.

These are our recommendations for the 4-to-6 age group:

Practice-to-game ratio: 1 or 2 to 1

Length of practices: 1 hour or shorter (longer if the kids ask to stay)

Playing time: equal for all players

Positions: players should get a chance to try all positions; with kids of this age, games are best with 4 to 6 players and a parent or coach playing first base; as the season progresses, make sure those players who get a chance to play first base can do so safely; players not on the field should be doing drills in the outfield.

Base distances: 40 to 50 feet

Pitching particulars: as the season progresses, the batting tee may be eliminated in favor of short tosses from a coach; be careful with this because some players won't be able to hit pitched balls; keep the batting tee handy for those players; always give players the choice of how they would like to hit.

Pitching distances: not applicable

Basic Practice Format

The key to running a successful practice, especially with the youngest group, is to keep kids active and provide a variety of activities to prevent boredom and horseplay. Developing different stations, creating small groups, and allowing kids to rotate frequently will allow you to maintain the kids' interest throughout an hour-long practice.

Practice Outline
for the 4-to-6 Age Group

5 min.   **Run the bases**

- Explain that first is the only base you can run past.
- Explain that you must touch the bases or be called out.
- Play follow the leader.

5 min.   **Stretch**

- Stretch in a circle around the pitcher's mound. The routine should be quick and simple.
- Lay out the day's practice plan.

30 min.   **Practice in stations, 10 min. per station and then rotate**

- Hitting off the tee and tossed balls
- Fielding and catching
- Throwing

15 min.   **Play a scrimmage or other instructional game**

5 min.   **Run the bases and review**

- Sprint around the bases. Incorporate races or chases.
- Let kids slide into home to finish.

For the 4-to-6 age group, 1 hour is the longest you'll want to practice, unless kids are asking for more. Some days you might want to cut practice off after 45 minutes. Other days the hour will fly by, and kids will want to stay longer. You should probably never keep them much past an hour, though; if they're having a great time when they leave, they'll be eager to come back for the next practice.

Running the Bases

How many times have you seen a coach send young kids out for a jog around the soccer field before practice? We see it with some frequency. But, really, 4-, 5-, and 6-year-olds don't know *how* to jog; plus, they don't need to. Most of them are going to sprint and render themselves out of commission for the next 15 minutes. A better idea is to have them run the bases just long enough to expend some excess energy. You can play follow the leader. Have them follow you from home to first (no passing the coach!), teaching them that it's okay to overrun first base, but if they try it on the other bases they can be tagged out. Then lead them all the way around the bases, having them make a proper turn (bow out gradually; the path should resemble a sickle) before touching each base, reinforcing that it's best to touch the inside of the base with either foot. You might also teach them how to run out a double or how to score from second on a hit. Keep the pace at a jog or slightly faster to start practice.

Follow a similar routine at the end of practice, but this time let kids sprint around the bases and slide into home plate. Kids love to get dirty on the ball field. Challenge them to beat you around the bases one time and then bring up the rear the next time, chasing them all the way around. Set up relay races. The racing and chasing aspect ensures they'll have fun with it. This is a great time to reinforce the direction that they are supposed to run after they hit the ball, which is one of the basic rules they'll need to learn early. This is also a good time to make sure the kids understand that they have to touch one base before running to the next or they will be called out.

Stretching

As we've mentioned, kids at this age don't need to stretch. They're loose all the time. This 5 minutes of stretching allows them to catch their breath and gives you a chance to prepare them for practice. Get them excited. Tell them they're going to get to hit a lot but will also practice throwing and catching. Always be positive and upbeat about what you'll cover in practice. The stretching routine also gets the kids used to the idea that stretching *is* important and should be done before any practice once they get a little older. Remember not to let your players stretch cold muscles. Make sure they have run a little before they stretch to get the blood flowing to the areas of the body they'll be stretching.

Practicing in Stations

This is where the small groups and rotations come into play. If you have a team of 12, you'll break them down into three groups of four. One group goes to home plate to work on hitting. Another group goes to right field to work on fielding and catching. A third group goes to left field to work on throwing. Each station lasts 10 minutes, and then groups rotate; the right-field group moves to left field, the left-field group moves to home plate, and the hitting group moves to right field.

Hitting Station

You want the stations to be active, so you won't spend much time teaching before you let them hit. Demonstrate what you expect them to do, and then have the kids stand in and take a few whacks at the

Hitting stations keep players active and often are the highlight of practice.

ball off the tee. Work with them to correct any flaws that prevent them from hitting the ball, but don't get too technical. Make sure players are using a bat they can handle. Let them hit and have fun. After each player has hit a few balls off the tee, try tossing a few pitched balls to them. Some kids won't be able to hit the thrown ball, and some will. For those who can't, bring the tee back out again so they end up feeling good about themselves. You might end the station with a quick hitting-for-distance contest using the tee. Or set up a point system for ground balls, line drives, and "home runs." Give the winners a piece of bubble gum or some other inexpensive prize.

Fielding and Catching Station

The basic fundamentals for fielding a ground ball—create a wide base with your feet, keep your butt down, and get your hands out in front—can be taught to any age group. It's okay to use heavier safety baseballs or real baseballs when teaching kids how to field ground balls, because these balls stay in the glove better when rolled. Coaches should *always* roll (not hit) ground balls to this age group and should try to get the balls to roll directly into the gloves. Teaching the concept of using the bare hand to hold the ball in the glove once it's fielded is important. Most kids won't have a glove that's broken in, nor will many of them possess the strength to squeeze their gloves enough to maintain control of the ball after catching it.

With very small groups at this age we recommend lining players up along the foul line so that they're all facing you and there's plenty of room in between each one. Have them all assume the ground ball fielding position and hold it while you go up and down the line, feeding them ground balls. Start slowly and then pick up the pace. Have each player toss you the ball after catching it. After a few times through, roll balls to different players at random. Then turn this into an elimination game in which those who catch the balls successfully stay in and those who miss sit down. Be *very* generous with how you judge this, however. The game should not be about winning and losing. It's about learning, concentrating, and developing motor skills. Balls can be rolled harder and from a greater distance as kids improve. As the season progresses, you can introduce more advanced players to the concept of backhanding a ball.

Catching a thrown or batted ball is one of the hardest motor skills for young children to develop. The issue is more about tracking than anything else. If you roll a ball toward toddlers, instead of tracking the ball and waiting for it to reach them before trying to stop it, they'll reach out and try to grab the ball at the last place they saw it. Inevitably, the ball scoots by the child.

For similar reasons, catching a ball out of the air is a difficult skill for kids to develop. The ability to catch comes much later for most children than hitting or throwing. There are many variables when it comes to catching: pointing the glove's fingers up on throws above the chest, turning the glove so the fingers point down for balls below the waist, catching in-between balls, and so on.

Kids generally shy away from things thrown at them, which is why it's best to use softer balls when teaching them to catch. At this age, with gloves yet to be broken in, the first concept to introduce to the kids is not to fear the ball. You can do this by having fun with them and playfully bouncing one of the softer balls off one of their heads so they can see it doesn't hurt. After that, line them up along the foul line similar to the ground ball station. Toss each player a soft ball so that it goes into the glove and have them cover the ball with the

 ## Other Ideas to Improve Tracking

Although it looks odd on a baseball field, using balloons, beach balls, or other bigger rubber or vinyl-covered balls at practice can be a good way to help kids work on their tracking skills. The balloons and bigger balls are easier to catch because of their size, and there's no fear of getting hurt. Balloons jump around all over the place, too, which means players have to really concentrate to track and catch them. If nothing else, this activity can be a fun diversion for your team.

You can create a catching progression using bigger and softer balls to reinforce the idea of catching with two hands out in front of the body. Start by using the soft rhino-skin balls used by physical education classes for dodge ball and similar games. Have the players drop their gloves and position their hands out in front of their bodies with their fingers up. Throw the ball pretty hard at each player until they can all catch the ball properly. Go up and down the line. Throw the ball above the chest every time. Then have them turn their fingers down to catch lower throws. After that, mix it up a bit, alternating high and low throws. Pick up the pace, going up and down the line quickly and challenging the kids to keep up with you. This improves their concentration and maintains their interest.

After a few more trips up and down the line, have them use their gloves the same way and throw a soft, smaller ball to them. As they improve, progress to soft baseballs, and eventually, to real baseballs. This activity can be turned into an elimination contest and should be done at every practice with this age group.

bare hand, introducing the concept of catching with two hands out in front of the body. Go through the line and then come back to the beginning. Each time through the line, toss the ball a little higher. They'll improve quickly to the point that you can eventually move them around a bit and they'll still be able to catch the ball.

Turn this activity into an elimination game, as you did at the ground ball station, allowing those who catch the balls successfully to stay in and having those who miss to sit down. Again, be generous in your judging, giving each player several chances before making anyone sit. By the end of the season, some kids will improve enough in their ability to track the ball that they'll be able to start catching thrown and hit balls with their fingers pointing up. As the season progresses, the kids can actually begin to play catch with one another.

Throwing Station

It's amazing to see how many kids, even older kids, don't throw properly. Throwing is a skill that should be worked on every day in practice by players of all ages. With the youngest players you don't want to get too technical, but you might be surprised at how much they can absorb.

Using softer balls or real baseballs (whichever you have enough of), have kids line up along the foul line, giving themselves plenty of space so they don't interfere with those next to them. Have them turn their bodies, point their front shoulders straight ahead, and raise their throwing arms so that the elbow is above the shoulder. Tell them over and over, "Turn, point the shoulder, elbow above the what?" and let them shout out an answer. Keep doing this every time. Then have them step with the nonthrowing-side foot toward the target and throw. Determine who threw the ball farthest and make a big deal out of it; then have them race to see who can retrieve their ball first and get back to the foul line. They'll love the competitive aspect of this activity.

Don't worry too much about proper grip at this age. It's a good idea to introduce the concept of the four-seam grip so that it's not foreign to the players as they get older, but developing proper mechanics is most important. Using two, three, or even four fingers to throw is acceptable. As the season progresses, concentrating more on the four-seam grip and its importance might be appropriate, but for now focus on teaching your players to throw the ball with the correct mechanics. In this age group you'll find a lot of kids who place their hand below the ball when they take it out of their glove and prepare to throw. Stop these players and explain to them the proper way to hold the ball. If you do this enough and keep reminding them, eventually it will sink in.

After a few throws, you can demonstrate how they can use their bodies to throw even farther. Throw one ball flat-footed so that it doesn't go too far. Then pick up a ball, shuffle your feet, and really let one fly. They'll be amazed at the difference. Have them try the same experiment and see which ball goes the farthest. Then have them race to retrieve their balls. Finally, have them all shuffle or run up and throw to see who can throw the farthest. Again, have them race to pick up their balls after the winner has been determined. As we mentioned earlier, you can have your kids play catch with each other later on in the season and maybe introduce a few of the more advanced throwing drills described in chapter 6.

Playing Scrimmages and Other Games

The one thing you'll learn quickly about baseball or T-ball for the 4-to-6 age group is that sometimes less is more. Many times, practices attended by fewer kids are more productive than those attended by the entire team. In a game situation, instead of having nine defensive players on the field, it often works better to have four, five, or six. Kids at this age can't hit the ball very far, so there's no need for outfielders, and when everyone is crammed into the infield there's no chance to learn about positional play. By putting four to six kids in the field, mixed in with parents, and having four to six kids on the opposing team, it becomes much easier to play a game in which the kids actually learn something. It's going to be really difficult to find a player who can play first base and catch throws consistently at this age. Consider playing a parent at first base so the fielders can begin to learn what it means to field a ball and throw to first for an out.

Taking the concept of scaled-down games even further, we recommend that leagues consider playing their games in this manner. Teams can divide into groups of four players. A group from one team is in the field, while the others are at the hitting, throwing, or fielding stations with another coach in the outfield. The team in the field stations a player at pitcher, second, third, and short, and a parent plays first base. The other team has a group of four hitting, with the others in stations in the outfield. Each player hits once, and then the other team's group hits. After one "inning" in which everyone hits, players rotate. Groups doing the stations come in to hit and play the field, while the ones who were hitting and fielding rotate to the stations. This activity can go on for a full hour, or even a little longer. Imagine how much more constructive and enjoyable this would be compared to 12 versus 12 T-ball. As the kids progress and improve their throwing and catching skills, the parent at first base can be replaced by one

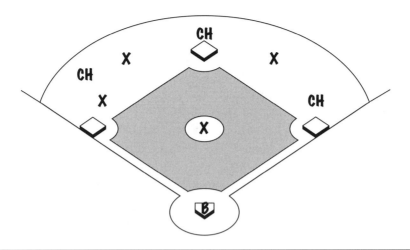

Modified game setup and positioning.

of the players. This format would be extremely beneficial for leagues that only play games and don't practice once the season begins.

If four to a side doesn't work well because of the number of players on a team, use five or six players instead. Just make sure the players are spaced out enough on the infield so they can begin to understand the concept of positional play (see the illustration above). Having a parent play first at the start of the season is critical because it allows the defensive team to field a hit ball and throw to someone who can catch it. When one of the kids is playing first, throws from the infielders are rarely caught, so very few outs are recorded. It also can be dangerous. If there's someone on first who can catch, the concept of recording the out at first base begins to make sense to the kids. It's important to stress to the fielders that if the ball is hit to their team-mate (or their buddy), they should let him or her field it. Sometimes it helps to station parents in between positions to help reinforce this concept. Don't let players leave their positions and wander past where the parents are standing.

If your league is not willing to try the scaled-down games, we recommend playing regular baseball rules: Record three outs and then switch sides. Allow runners to try for doubles and triples when they hit the ball far enough. Many times, when leagues for this age group play their games, everyone bats in every inning, and each batter stops at first after hitting the ball. Combine this with the fact that every player is on the field defensively and that the kids often jump on each other and try to wrestle batted balls away from each other, and what you end up with is very little learning about how the game should be played. Practice is the best time for kids to learn the game. Take advantage of that opportunity by being creative with your practices—and push your leagues to adopt the game-day format we have recommended.

Another way to teach the game of baseball to younger players is to use other games that they already know and understand to teach concepts about baseball. You can get creative with this, but here's one example. A concept that's often overlooked at the youngest ages is that of tagging a player to get an out. There's a simple way to teach this: by playing a game of tag on the baseball field. Explain to your players that they're safe whenever they're standing on a base and that when they leave the base they can be tagged out by a person with the ball. Designate one player as "it" and put him or her on the pitcher's mound. Spread out the rest of the team by stationing several players at each base. Yell, "Go!" and have the kids all try to run to the next base while the player with the ball tries to tag someone. Whoever gets tagged becomes the new "it." After you're done playing, gather everyone together and explain that in a baseball or T-ball game you can get runners out by tagging them with the ball. Remind them of this during games when runners are on base.

Think of some other games that might translate to baseball and help young players understand the rules. Try them out and let us know how they work. Get creative! Fun and learning are a winning combination.

9

Practice Particulars for Ages 7 to 9

Most kids in the 7-to-9 age group will play some form of baseball in which coaches or pitching machines are the pitchers. At the younger end of this spectrum, a transition from coaches or machines to other kids pitching might occur at some point in the season. Other programs stick with coaches and machines as pitchers for the duration. By the time players reach the age of 9, they want to take their at-bats against kids their own age, and most players want to try their hands at pitching. It's easy to give in to these preferences to make the kids happy, but doing so can be dangerous. The beauty of coach- and machine-pitch games is that the games are fast-paced. There are a lot of strikes and a lot of balls put into play. The batters become better hitters, the defensive players get more repetitions, and nobody gets bored. Everyone improves, which should be the ultimate goal at this level. We're not saying we shouldn't try to appease the players, but if the kids are going to pitch, limits need to be set on the number of walks and hit batters allowed per inning. Coaches need to be directed as to when it's the proper time to step in and take over the pitching. The kids might want to try pitching and hitting against each other, but no one has fun when it's ball 4, ball 8, ball 12, and so on.

Many youth teams in the 7-to-9 age group will practice once a week and play once a week. If that's the case with your team, you can find a practice that you like in this chapter or alternate using one of the three practices each week before starting over in week four. There are some teams in this age group that will practice twice a week and play once or twice a week, and it's becoming more and more common at this age to see travel teams that practice three or more times a week before their seasons start. Unfortunately, however, once teams start their seasons, practices often go by the wayside in favor of games. For developmental purposes, we recommend at least a 2:1 ratio of practices to games throughout the season, although 3:1 would be even better.

If your league doesn't provide a field to practice on once your season begins, try to find a field somewhere to practice on at least once a week. Your players won't improve as quickly if they don't get the repetitions that practice provides, and they'll be less likely to absorb lessons from their games if situations aren't discussed in a practice setting.

If you can practice more than once per week, simply use each practice once and then start back with practice plan 1. For the most part, practices at this age group should not extend much past an hour unless the kids really want to stay longer. If practice goes long, make sure to choose some of the fun drills from the Practice Planner.

Accounting for Differences in Interest and Skill Level

Coaches of teams in the 7-to-9 age group will quickly discover that they're dealing with kids of varying interest and skill levels. Some kids will have fallen in love with the game and will bring an intensity and focus to the field characteristic of a much older player. These players will show a desire to improve, a thirst to learn, and a competitive instinct that can't be taught. They'll be a joy to coach, and their intensity will bring a smile to your face.

Most players will behave like typical 7- to 9-year-olds. One minute they'll approach the game like a pro, and the next minute they'll be rolling around and playing in the dirt. Sometimes they'll listen and do exactly what you ask, and other times they'll be watching the ice cream truck while you're trying to teach. One minute they'll be into the game and cheering on their teammates, and the next they will be playing tag behind the dugout.

Sometimes peer pressure takes care of these situations. The more intense players get frustrated with the lack of structure and attention and will reprimand their teammates, who might fall into line. More often, however, the more serious players are in the minority, so you must create an environment that holds your players' attention and establish game-day rules to keep things under control.

Once again, practices should feature small groups and stations, with players rotating to new activities every 10 minutes or so. Incorporate games and contests into the drills to make them less tedious and more fun. Provide opportunities for players to run (baserunning or tag games) and to get dirty (sliding). These are especially good activities to turn to if practice becomes boring. If players get distracted during practice, tell them that if they pay attention they'll get a chance to slide, run the bases, or participate in games or contests later—but *only* if they pay attention. Provide rewards for good behavior in the forms of activities that excite the players and keep them in line. Generally, if you keep the kids active and move them into a new activity every 10 minutes or so, it's much easier to maintain their energy and attention.

Multiple coaches and small groups keep kids active.

When it comes to game time, you can't have players straying far from the bench area. If no controls are in place, injuries to players and spectators are much more likely to happen away from the field and the bench than on the field or in the dugout. Young kids playing catch or swinging bats near a group of spectators or siblings is a recipe for disaster. The best way to handle this sort of situation is to allow one parent—and only one—into the bench area to be the bench manager for that game. Players who leave the bench area without permission risk losing playing time. The bench manager's job is to keep the bench area safe, involve players in the game through discussions about what's happening on the field, ensure that players know the batting order and are wearing a batting helmet before they go on deck, and encourage players to support their teammates.

When constructing practices for this age group, another key concern is the wide range of differences in ability and physical maturity of your players. In some leagues, 7- and 8-year-olds will be playing together. You might have a 50-pound 7-year-old competing against an 8-year-old who weighs nearly 100 pounds. The same type of differences can arise when 8- and 9-year-olds are grouped together. Many times, the biggest kids are not the best, but if you run across a really big, strong kid who is skilled and mix him or her in with some smaller players who aren't as skilled, unsafe playing conditions can result. In such instances, it's acceptable to consider allowing a kid to play in an older age group. If the kid's mental *and* physical capacities are more of a match with an older age group, by all means that player should be allowed to play at the next level.

To deal with the size and skill differences, it's best to match players of similar size and skill level when creating your smaller practice groups. You can tailor the level of instruction and types of drills to fit each group's ability level. This will keep the practice more interesting for players of all skill levels and allow you to better address the areas each particular group needs to focus on. The higher-skilled players will remain interested and feel challenged. They'll continue to improve throughout the season. The less-skilled players will improve more rapidly in the basic fundamentals they need to compete safely with the other players.

The goals presented here are team goals that you should strive to achieve as a unit. But keep in mind the need to involve all of your players and make them excited about coming to practice. Some players might advance beyond the basic drills to the point that they're ready to handle more advanced concepts. Others might need to keep working on the basics. Your challenge as a coach at this level is to adapt each part of your practice to the needs of the group of players involved. This might mean that groups are doing different drills at the hitting station, which can take a little more thought and work on your part. The end result—seeing every player on your team improve and begin to develop a love for the game—is well worth the extra effort.

Keep in mind the goals for this age group as presented in chapter 3. These will be your priorities for the season:

1. Learning the basic rules—force outs; tagging up; baserunning (when you don't have to run; not running into or past teammates on the basepaths); balls and strikes.

2. Throwing mechanics—introduce the four-seam grip; point the front shoulder, step, and throw; introduce the concept of generating momentum toward the target and following the throw.

3. Catching and fielding—thrown and hit balls; fingers up versus fingers down; see the glove and the ball; use two hands; forehands and backhands; introduce the underhand flip; first-base fundamentals; crossover and drop steps.

4. Hitting—choosing the right bat; proper grip; hitting pitched balls; introduce drill work (tee, soft toss, short toss).

5. Learning positional play—learn the positions and the areas each player should cover; cover the nearest base when the ball is not hit to you; basics of cutoffs and relays.

These are our recommendations for the 7-to-9 age group:

Practice-to-game ratio: 2 or 3 to 1

Length of practices: 1 hour (no more than 1 hour and 15 minutes, no matter what)

Playing time: equal for all players

Positions: players should get a chance to try all positions throughout the season; make sure those players who get a chance to play first base can do so safely; don't force players who aren't interested in pitching to pitch, regardless of their arm strength.

Base distances: 60 feet

Pitching particulars: coaches or machines for age 7; for age 8, coaches or machines for half the season and kids with strict walk and hit-batter restrictions for half the season; for age 9, kids with strict walk and hit-batter restrictions.

Pitching distances: 40 feet for ages 7 and 8 (although kids really shouldn't pitch at age 7); 46 feet for age 9

Three-Day Sample Practice Guide

Practice Plan Day 1

5 min.   **Dynamic warm-up**

- Skipping, high-knee skipping, high-knee jogging, bounding, backward running, jogging

5 min.   **Baserunning**

- Big League Baserunning (controlled, follow the leader)

5 min.   **Stretching**

- Hamstrings, quads, groin, back, shoulders, triceps

10 min.   **Throwing**

- Power Position Drill with coaches (5 min.); with teammates after a few sessions
- One-Knee Drill with coaches (5 min.); with teammates after a few sessions
- As season progresses, you can replace these drills with playing catch and any of the fun throwing drills from groupings 1, 2, or 3. Pitchers can do drills from grouping 4.

30 min.   **Stations (3 groups, 10 min. each station)**

- Hitting (Tee Work, Soft Toss); as the season progresses, you can substitute any fun or regular hitting drill from groupings 1, 2, 3, or 4.
- Infield and throwing (Rolled Ground Balls, Throwing After the Catch Drill); as the season progresses, you can substitute any fun or regular infield or throwing drills from groupings 1, 2, 3, or 4.
- Outfield (Thrown Fly Balls; use sponge balls or soft baseballs until skills are developed); as the season progresses, you can substitute any fun or regular outfield drills from groupings 1 or 4.

10 min.   **Basic rules session or any fun drill from groupings 1, 2, or 3**

5 min.   **Baserunning**

- Big League Baserunning or any fun baserunning drills from grouping 1 (run hard)

Three-Day Sample Practice Guide

Practice Plan Day 2

5 min.   **Dynamic warm-up (same as day 1)**

- Skipping, high-knee skipping, high-knee jogging, bounding, backward running

5 min.   **Baserunning (same as day 1)**

- Big League Baserunning (controlled, follow the leader)

5 min.   **Stretching (same as day 1)**

- Hamstrings, quads, groin, back, shoulders, triceps

15 min.   **Throwing and catching**

- Power Position Drill with coaches (5 min.); with teammates after a few sessions
- One-Knee Drill with coaches (5 min.); with teammates after a few sessions
- Catch coach's throws with two hands in front (5 min.); use bigger balls, Lite Flite balls, or soft baseballs.
- As season progresses, you can replace these drills with playing catch and any of the fun throwing drills from groupings 1, 2, or 3. Pitchers can do drills from grouping 4.

30 min.   **Stations (3 groups, 10 min. each station)**

- Hitting (Short Toss From the Front); as the season progresses, you can substitute any fun or regular hitting drill from groupings 1, 2, 3, or 4.
- Infield and throwing (review fielding ground balls and throwing after the catch; include backhand drills); as the season progresses, you can substitute any fun or regular infield or throwing drills from groupings 1, 2, 3, or 4.
- Outfield (Thrown Fly Balls, Thrown or Machine Ground Balls); as the season progresses, you can substitute fun or regular outfield drills from groupings 1 or 4.

15 min.   **Controlled game, game situations, or rules session**

(continued)

Three-Day Sample Practice Guide *(continued)*

Practice Plan Day 3

5 min.   **Dynamic warm-up (same as day 1)**

- Skipping, high-knee skipping, high-knee jogging, bounding, backward running

5 min.   **Baserunning (same as day 1)**

- Big League Baserunning (controlled, follow the leader)

5 min.   **Stretching (same as day 1)**

- Hamstrings, quads, groin, back, shoulders, triceps

10 min.   **Throwing and catching**

- Players play catch; stress mechanics and catching with two hands in front of body.
- Play Twenty-One.
- As season progresses, you can replace these drills with regular or fun throwing drills from groupings 1, 2, or 3. Pitchers can do drills from grouping 4.

30 min.   **Stations (3 groups, 10 min. each station)**

- Hitting (Free Hitting or Line Drive Home Run Derby); as the season progresses, you can substitute any fun or regular hitting drill from groupings 1, 2, 3, or 4.
- Infield and throwing (review backhands, High Five Drill); as the season progresses, you can substitute any fun or regular infield or throwing drills from groupings 1, 2, 3, or 4.
- Outfield (Crossover Step Drill, Pass Patterns); as the season progresses, you can substitute any fun or regular outfield drills from groupings 1 or 4.

15 min.   **Controlled game or any combination of fun drills from groupings 1, 2, or 3**

10

Practice Particulars for Ages 10 to 12

When players reach the 10-to-12 age group, it starts to become apparent which kids are suited to certain positions. The players with the best arms gravitate toward the pitching mound, shortstop, and third base, and kids who like to catch might show up with their own gear. That said, this age group remains very much developmental. Some kids are much more developed physically than others, but at some point over the next few years the less-developed players will catch up. With this in mind, we recommend exposing players to as many positions as they're willing to try.

Players from 10 to 12 seem to get bigger and stronger each year. We believe that most players at this age have outgrown the traditional 60-foot diamonds with the 46-foot pitching distance. This certainly is true for the 11-to-12 age group. Some 10-year-olds might be better suited for the smaller fields, but there's little question that there should be a transition to the bigger diamond for ages 11 and 12. This move is extremely beneficial for players as they progress up the youth baseball ladder and encounter the transition to even bigger fields during the subsequent years. The bigger diamond lends itself to a game that more closely resembles real baseball, complete with doubles, triples, and double plays. This type of game, which should also include leading and stealing, better prepares players for their baseball futures.

Placing Players in Positions to Succeed

As players enter the 10-to-12 age group, they are probably beginning to gravitate toward the positions at which they have the most success. Being successful is fun for kids, so it's natural that they want to play those positions most often. As kids get older, the games start to become a little more serious, and at some point coaches begin to base their decisions about positions and playing time more on merit. Always keep in mind that kids mature at different rates emotionally, mentally, and physically. Yes, more of your decisions might be based on skill level, but you want to allow your players to try any position that interests them.

Your top objective remains to develop well-rounded baseball players. Discouraging a kid who wants to try shortstop might squash his or her enthusiasm for the game and drive him or her away from the sport. Exposing players to more positions helps them develop a better overall understanding of the game and makes them more valuable to their teams as they grow older. Allowing kids to try a position in practice and then never giving them a chance to play that position in a game can be confusing and demoralizing. The worst thing you can do is to get someone's hopes up and then fail to give him or her an opportunity. Kids in this age group are still developing their knowledge base and skill level, so if you're going to have them work on the skills needed to play every position, as we recommend, it only makes sense to give them opportunities to try what they've learned in a game setting.

At this level of play you're going to be able to determine, for the most part, who your best players are at each position. These are usually the players who are the most comfortable and relaxed in game situations. Other players need repetitions in practice to develop the same comfort level, so it's imperative to ensure that your kids get equal repetitions at the positions that interest them. Usually your best players can both pitch and play other positions, so focus on developing players who can fill in capably when one of your infielders is on the mound. You don't want to place an unprepared player into a game situation, because the inevitable result is failure. With small rosters, injuries, vacations, and so on, you never know what lineup combination you might have to use. So be sure to prepare your players to take on as many roles as possible. Otherwise, you're placing them in no-win situations in which failure is the most likely outcome. As we've said, repeated failures can turn a player off to baseball altogether.

As players get older, more specialization naturally takes place. Make sure any players you see as pitchers have the desire to pitch.

If you have players whom you envision as potential pitchers, your first step should be to make sure these players are interested in pitching. Pitcher is the most pressure-filled position on the baseball field, so putting a player out on the mound who doesn't want to be there can be disastrous. It also isn't fair to throw a kid into the fire if he or she hasn't practiced his or her pitching enough to gain some confidence on the mound. Find out at your first practice who's interested in pitching, and work with those kids throughout the season, whether you see them as potential pitchers or not. Some kids who you think are natural pitchers because they have strong arms won't have the emotional makeup or desire to pitch. Others with less physical ability will turn into bulldogs who get batters out by throwing strikes. Some players might take two or three years (or longer) to develop into pitchers, but they have a better chance for success if you begin working with them at an early age.

You never know what's going to happen during your season, so having as many players as you can prepared to assume a variety of roles is important to your team's success and the players' overall development and enjoyment of the game. Make sure that your players spend time working on all of the game's fundamentals during practices. Doing so substantially improves the chances that you're putting your players in positions in which they can succeed. The more success your players experience, the more they'll enjoy the sport, and that should keep them coming back for more.

Keeping Up With the Rules of the Game

The 10-to-12 age group is when kids begin to get serious about pitching. Most leagues for 10-year-old players don't permit stealing, so when leads and steals enter the picture at ages 11 and 12, young pitchers must adapt to the concepts of holding runners on and throwing from the stretch. As 10-year-olds, pitchers should be made aware of the differences between throwing from the wind-up and the stretch so they're prepared as they move up to the next age group. Pitchers at ages 11 and 12 should practice throwing from both the stretch and the wind-up during preseason practices. They should be placed in gamelike situations in which they have to hold runners on base, field comebackers, and cover first on ground balls to the right side. Working on these situations with your pitchers also lets you work with baserunners on taking leads and stealing bases. In addition, you'll start to find out which, if any, of your players are capable of being catchers (blocking pitches, throwing out runners, and so on). Again, you want to put your players in positions to succeed. As games become more competitive, teams begin trying to bunt more often, so learning to field bunts is also important for 10- to 12-year-old pitchers.

Pitchers at this age can begin doing some of the pitching drills from both the wind-up and the stretch and start learning to throw two-seam fastballs and change-ups. More than likely, you'll have several players on your team who are interested in pitching, so think seriously about incorporating a pitching station for everyone into your practices. This will ensure that you have as many prepared pitchers as possible (and for those who really don't want to pitch, it's always helpful to work on proper throwing mechanics). One of the most demoralizing situations for a young player is to be asked to pitch and not be comfortable on the mound. Nothing's worse than standing on the rubber, being called for a balk, watching runners advance, and having no idea what just happened.

Preparing for the Big Field

Players in this age group, for the most part, are getting ready to move up to a regulation-sized diamond when they turn 13, so you want to help them develop aspects of their games to ease that transition. Focus on throwing drills, especially the long-toss drills that help build arm strength.

Infielders should focus on developing their ability to backhand ground balls; if they try to get in front of every ball hit to the backhand side and end up catching those balls while moving away from first base, they're going to have trouble making an accurate, on-time throw to first as they get older and the distance of the throw increases.

Finally, all players should work on patience when hitting. Pitchers are going to start throwing more off-speed and breaking pitches as they get older, which will make batters who transfer their weight to the front foot too quickly susceptible. In addition, the pitching distance will soon lengthen from 46 or 50 feet to 60 feet, 6 inches, which means hitters will have more time to decide whether or not to swing. Batters accustomed to rushing forward to catch up with faster pitches will find themselves way out in front and unable to generate maximum bat speed. Short Toss From the Front and Lob Toss are good drills to assist young hitters who are having these problems.

Striking the Balance

Most youth teams in the 10-to-12 age group will have one or two practices and two or more games per week. Travel teams at this level might practice three or more days during the preseason and play four or more times a week. On occasion, you'll find leagues that play up to three games a week with no practices. Games are fun for kids, but the lack of practices during the season can be detrimental to their development, so at this age we still recommend a minimum 2-to-1 ratio of practices to games (3 to 1 is even better.) If your league can't provide a practice field at least once a week, do your best to find one on your own. The three days of practice we suggest in this chapter might help you plan out an entire week or might carry over into the next week. Maintain these formats throughout your season, charting your team's progress and using the appropriate drills as players develop their skills.

When planning your practices, always keep in mind the goals for this age group as established in chapter 3. These will be your priorities for the season:

1. Learning the basic rules—infield fly rule; balks.

2. Baserunning—leads; steals; extra-base hits.

3. Pitching and throwing mechanics—wind-up versus stretch; four-seam grip; shuffle, throw, follow; pitcher covering first.

4. Hitting—repetitions; drill work (tee, soft toss, short toss, stickball, lob toss, one-arm drill); bunting.

5. Learning team fundamentals—cutoffs and relays; basic bunt defenses; basic first-and-third situations; underhand flip (box drill) and double plays; defending the steal; infield and outfield communication and priorities.

These are our recommendations for the 10-to-12 age group:

Practice-to-game ratio: 2 or 3 to 1

Length of practices: can be extended to 1 hour and 15 minutes or more (no longer than 90 minutes)

Playing time: equal for all players

Positions: players should get to try any positions they desire; positions will naturally become more specialized based on player development and ability.

Base distances: 70 feet (60 feet for most 10-year-olds)

Pitching particulars: kids pitch; limit or exclude breaking balls.

Pitching distances: 46 feet for age 10; 50 feet for ages 11 and 12

Three-Day Sample Practice Guide

Practice Plan Day 1

5 min.   **Dynamic warm-up**

- Skipping, high-knee skipping, high-knee jogging, bounding, backward running, jogging
- Big League Baserunning or general baserunning can be done as jogging.

5 min.   **Stretching**

- Hamstrings, quads, groin, back, shoulders, triceps

10 min.   **Throwing and catching**

- One-Knee Drill with teammates (4 min.)
- Power Position Drill with teammates (4 min.)
- Play catch or play Twenty-One with teammates (2 min.).
- Emphasize proper mechanics and accuracy on each throw; focus on catching the ball out in front with two hands.

20 min.   **Team fundamentals**

- Choose from cutoffs and relays, first-and-third offense and defense, defending the steal (if your league permits stealing), infield and outfield communication and priorities.

30 min.   **Stations (3 groups, 10 min. each station)**

- Hitting (Tee Work, Soft Toss); any hitting drill from groupings 1, 3, 4, or 5 can be substituted as the season progresses.
- Infield and throwing (Rolled Ground Balls, Throwing After the Catch Drill); any infield or throwing drills from groupings 1, 3, 4, or 5 can be substituted as the season progresses.
- Outfield (Thrown Fly Balls; use soft baseballs until skills are developed); any outfield drills from groupings 1, 4, or 5 can be substituted as the season progresses.

5 min.   **Baserunning**

- Big League Baserunning (full speed) or another baserunning drill from grouping 1

(continued)

Three-Day Sample Practice Guide (continued)

Practice Plan Day 2

5 min. **Dynamic warm-up (same as day 1)**
- Skipping, high-knee skipping, high-knee jogging, bounding, backward running, jogging
- Big League Baserunning or general baserunning can be done as jogging.

5 min. **Stretching (same as day 1)**
- Hamstrings, quads, groin, back, shoulders, triceps

10 min. **Throwing and catching**
- Review One-Knee Drill and Power Position Drill (5 min.).
- Play catch or play Twenty-One with teammates (5 min.).
- Emphasize proper mechanics and accuracy on each throw; focus on catching the ball out in front with two hands.
- Any throwing drill from groupings 1, 3, 4, or 5 can be substituted as the season progresses.
- Pitchers can work on throwing and pitching drills from groupings 4 or 5.

20 min. **Team fundamentals**
- Choose from cutoffs and relays, first-and-third offense and defense, defending the steal (if your league permits stealing), infield and outfield communication and priorities.

30 min. **Stations (3 groups, 10 min. each station)**
- Hitting (Short Toss From the Front); any hitting drill from groupings 1, 3, 4, or 5 can be substituted as the season progresses.
- Infield and throwing (review; backhand drills; High Five Drill); any infield or throwing drills from groupings 1, 3, 4, or 5 can be substituted as the season progresses.
- Outfield (review; Thrown or Machine Ground Balls; Communication Drill); any outfield drills from groupings 1, 4, or 5 can be substituted as the season progresses.

5 min. **Baserunning**
- Big League Baserunning (full speed) or another baserunning drill from grouping 1

Three-Day Sample Practice Guide

Practice Plan Day 3

5 min. **Dynamic warm-up (same as day 1)**
- Skipping, high-knee skipping, high-knee jogging, bounding, backward running, jogging
- Big League Baserunning or general baserunning can be done as jogging.

5 min. **Stretching (same as day 1)**
- Hamstrings, quads, groin, back, shoulders, triceps

10 min. **Throwing and catching**
- Other throwing games
- Emphasize proper mechanics and accuracy on each throw; focus on catching the ball out in front with two hands.
- Any throwing drills from groupings 1, 3, 4, or 5 can be used as the season progresses.
- Pitchers can work on throwing drills from groupings 4 or 5.

30 min. **Stations (3 groups, 10 min. each station)**
- Hitting (Free Hitting); any hitting drill from groupings 1, 3, 4, or 5 can be substituted as the season progresses.
- Infield and throwing (Box Drill or 4-6/6-4 Drill with First Base Drill); any infield or throwing drills from groupings 1, 3, 4, or 5 can be substituted as the season progresses.
- Outfield (Crossover Step Drill, Pass Patterns); any outfield drills from groupings 1, 4, or 5 can be substituted as the season progresses.

30 min. **Controlled game, soft toss game or T-ball game, or game situations**

5 min. **Baserunning**
- Big League Baserunning (full speed) or another baserunning drill from grouping 1

11

Practice Particulars for Ages 13 to 14

The 13-to-14 age group is a crucial one for the future of baseball, because traditionally it has been the group experiencing the greatest dropoff in participation. This is the age at which most players move to the regulation-sized diamond with 90-foot bases and a 60-foot, 6-inch pitching distance. Because of the way many youth programs are structured, kids often are asked to go from 60-foot bases and 46-foot pitching distances to a big league–sized playing surface. This expectation places a tremendous strain on players, most of whom aren't physically prepared to make such a huge jump. This is why we're hoping that more leagues for 11- and 12-year-olds will further the current trend of having their kids play on 70-foot diamonds. In a perfect world, there would be one additional intermediate field size between the 70- and 90-foot diamonds, but the trend toward 70-foot fields at the 11- and 12-year-old levels should somewhat ease the transition to regulation-sized diamonds.

Adjusting to the Big Field

As players progress to this age group, they need to focus even more on improving throwing mechanics and building arm strength. As players get older, practices get longer, and kids are forced to throw more often from longer distances. Making sure the elbow is above the shoulder, stressing the importance of generating momentum toward the target, following the throw, and long tossing are quite important at this stage of development. Some skills that can be avoided on smaller fields, such as backhanding ground balls, also become essential for this age group because of the need to get rid of the ball more quickly as the distance of the throws increases. When players attempt to get in front of a ground ball hit to the backhand side, many times they'll have to take a couple of hops or steps away from first base after catching the ball to stop their momentum. This lengthens the distance of the throw to first and also increases the amount of time it takes to deliver the ball. Both of these factors work against fielders as they attempt to get runners out.

Another key area of concern at this age level is the pitcher versus batter match-up. In preceding years, pitchers have a distinct advantage throwing from as close as 46 feet and no farther away than 50 feet. Harder-throwing pitchers often can dominate hitters at these distances using fastballs that require quicker reactions than are required of big league hitters. Some pitches thrown at the shorter distances can be equivalent to pitches exceeding 100 miles per hour from the 60-foot, 6-inch distance. To catch up, hitters often cheat and learn to shift their weight to the front foot early and to hit with a quick flick swing. When pitchers move to the 60-foot, 6-inch distance, that advantage is nullified, causing the hitters who cheat to get their weight out on the front foot so early that they have trouble generating power and become susceptible to off-speed and breaking pitches. Hitting drills should be geared toward patience and a proper weight shift that includes a short, soft stride. Pitchers should continue building arm strength by throwing a lot of fastballs and learning the importance of throwing and long tossing between game appearances.

Learning to Play the Game the Right Way

We hope by this point that most players who have kept playing the game have developed many of the basic fundamental skills required to enjoy at least some level of success. Players are emotionally mature

Players of all ages need to continue mastering the fundamental skills.

enough to handle a tryout or evaluation situation and accept whatever role is assigned to them by the coach. Physically, they're at a point at which they can throw a little harder, run a little faster, and handle the bat a little better. You can spend more time on developing team fundamentals and strategies, which are necessary for success and which players will need to understand if they are to continue playing as the game becomes more serious and competitive.

Practices should focus more on creating gamelike situations that might arise or that were mishandled in previous contests. Players are mature enough to understand the concepts of sacrifice bunts and productive outs. They should use hitting drills and batting practice to become more complete hitters, developing the ability to execute the hit and run and move runners over. Pitchers can begin to focus more on concepts such as holding runners, executing pickoff plays, and throwing specific pitches to locations based on game situations.

Still, with all of that said, the game most often comes down to who can throw and catch the best. Team fundamentals, specialty work, and game situations should never be practiced at the expense of the basic fundamentals. Spend time at each practice covering the fundamental skills of throwing, catching, and fielding. If your team can't handle the basics, trying to teach them the more advanced and team concepts is a waste of time. At this age level, a good mixture of individual and team fundamentals along with staged game situations is best.

Keep in mind that although your players are maturing rapidly, they're still kids. Baseball is a game and should be fun, so always do your best to create a light, enjoyable atmosphere. Small groups, timed stations, and contests are always a sure bet to make practices more interesting.

Practices at this age group can approach two hours, but monitor this closely. If players are having a rough day on the field, adjust your practice time or plan accordingly. Because of the dropoff in participation that occurs at this age group, most kids still playing baseball are fairly serious about the sport. Most will have figured out which positions they're best suited for and will naturally gravitate toward those spots. Remember that at this level you're still developing players for high school teams, so winning should take a backseat to providing developmental opportunities and keeping the game fun. Make it your goal to ensure that everyone on your team continues playing the game.

Following the basic formats presented here can get you started and get you through a series of practices. But, as your team progresses, make sure that you use our entire menu of drills within these formats to cover all aspects of the game while keeping the practices interesting and enjoyable. When planning your practices, always keep in mind the goals for this age group as established in chapter 3. These will be your priorities for the season:

1. Throwing mechanics and pitching—emphasis on generating momentum toward the target and following the throw (larger field); breaking balls; change-ups; pitching mechanics and using the body effectively (longer distance); pickoff mechanics; flatwork (drills); introduction to long toss.

2. Hitting—introduce situational hitting (inside-out swing; hitting behind runners; hit and run; productive outs); sacrifice bunting versus bunting for a hit; understanding the count.

3. Baserunning—first-and-third situations; steal breaks; delayed steals; reading situations and reacting to them.

4. Fielding—generating momentum back toward the target on throws when necessary; crossover and drop steps; backhands and when to use them; double-play depth; pitcher covering first; infield communication.

5. Learning team fundamentals—pickoff plays; full bunt defenses; full first-and-third defenses; pop-up and fly ball priorities; double plays and underhand flips.

These are our recommendations for the 13-to-14 age group:

Practice-to-game ratio: 2 or 3 to 1

Length of practices: up to 2 hours (mix in shorter practices when necessary)

Playing time: equal for all players (more serious teams may move *slightly* away from this)

Positions: players become more specialized, but don't deprive anyone of opportunities.

Base distances: 90 feet (75- or 80-foot intermediate distance would be ideal)

Pitching particulars: kids pitch; continue to limit breaking balls.

Pitching distance: 60 feet, 6 inches (54 feet for intermediate fields)

Three-Day Sample Practice Guide

Practice Plan Day 1

5 min.   **Dynamic warm-up**

- Skipping, high-knee skipping, high-knee jogging, bounding, backward running, jogging

5 min.   **Stretching**

- Hamstrings, quads, groin, back, shoulders, triceps

10 min.   **Throwing**

- One-Knee Drill with teammates (early in season)
- Power Position Drill with teammates (early in season)
- Play catch or play Twenty-One with teammates.
- Any throwing or pitching drills from groupings 1, 4, or 5 can be substituted as the season progresses.
- Emphasize long tossing throughout the season.

20 min.   **Infield and outfield work**

- Rolled Ground Balls, Throwing After the Catch Drill, Hitting Ground Balls, Thrown Fly Balls, Rolled or Machine Ground Balls, Hit Fly Balls or Machine Fly Balls

20 min.   **Team fundamentals**

- Choose from cutoffs and relays, pickoff plays, first-and-third offense and defense, full bunt defenses, pop-up and fly ball priorities, and defending steals.

60 min.   **Hitting stations, 15 min. per station**

- Soft Toss, Tee Work, Short Toss From the Front, Free Hitting
- Any hitting drills from groupings 1, 4, or 5 can be substituted as the season progresses.
- Infielders and outfielders can take more ground balls and fly balls during this time slot. Pitchers can get in bullpen throwing or do flatwork (pitching and throwing drills from groupings 4 or 5).

10 min.   **Pitcher's fielding practice (PFP) and Big League Baserunning**

- Pitcher Covering First Base Drill, Comebacker Drill, Bunt Drill

Three-Day Sample Practice Guide

Practice Plan Day 2

5 min.   **Dynamic warm-up (same as day 1)**
- Skipping, high-knee skipping, high-knee jogging, bounding, backward running, jogging

5 min.   **Stretching (same as day 1)**
- Hamstrings, quads, groin, back, shoulders, triceps

10 min.   **Throwing**
- One-Knee Drill with teammates (early in season)
- Power Position Drill with teammates (early in season)
- Play catch, play Twenty-One, or long toss with teammates.
- Any throwing or pitching drills from groupings 1, 4, or 5 can be substituted as the season progresses.
- Emphasize long tossing throughout the season.

20 min.   **Infield and outfield work**
- Backhand Throwing Drill, 4-6/6-4 Drill, First Base Drill, Hitting Ground Balls, Thrown Fly Balls, Rolled or Machine Ground Balls, Hit Fly Balls or Machine Fly Balls, Communication Drill, Crossover Step Drill
- Any infield drill from groupings 1, 4, or 5 can be substituted as the season progresses.

20 min.   **Team fundamentals**
- Choose from cutoffs and relays, pickoff plays, first-and-third offense and defense, full bunt defenses, pop-up and fly ball priorities, and defending steals.

60 min.   **Hitting stations, 15 min. per station**
- Short Toss From the Front, One-Arm Drill, Lob Toss, Stickball Drill, Free Hitting
- Any hitting drills from groupings 1, 4, or 5 can be substituted as the season progresses.
- Infielders and outfielders can take more ground balls and fly balls during this time slot. Pitchers can get in bullpen throwing or do flatwork (pitching and throwing drills from groupings 4 or 5).

10 min.   **Pitcher's fielding practice (PFP) and Big League Baserunning**
- Pitcher Covering First Base Drill, Comebacker Drill, Bunt Drill

(continued)

Three-Day Sample Practice Guide *(continued)*

Practice Plan Day 3

5 min. **Dynamic warm-up (same as day 1)**
- Skipping, high-knee skipping, high-knee jogging, bounding, backward running, jogging

5 min. **Stretching (same as day 1)**
- Hamstrings, quads, groin, back, shoulders, triceps

10 min. **Throwing**
- Play catch, play Twenty-One, or long toss with teammates.
- Other throwing games (optional)
- Any throwing or pitching drills from groupings 1, 4, or 5 can be substituted as the season progresses.
- Emphasize long tossing throughout the season.

20 min. **Infield and outfield work**
- Box Drill, backhand drills, Hitting Ground Balls, Backhand Throwing Drill, Crossover Step Drill, Drop Step Drill, Pass Patterns, Fence Drill
- Any infield drill from groupings 1, 4, or 5 can be substituted as the season progresses.
- Drills can be turned into contests on the third or final day of a week.

20 min. **Team fundamentals**
- Choose from cutoffs and relays, pickoff plays, first-and-third offense and defense, full bunt defenses, pop-up and fly ball priorities, and defending steals.

60 min. **Game situations, controlled scrimmage, soft toss game, or T-ball game**

10 min. **Big League Baserunning**

12

Practice Particulars for Ages 15+

It stands to reason that most baseball players still participating in the sport beyond the age of 15 are at least somewhat serious about the game. These players have figured out which positions are best for them and have put time and energy into developing their skills at these positions. Players have also matured enough emotionally to understand and accept their roles within the framework of the team. High school coaches are paid to win games, and summer league coaches are usually trying to win and help their players get seen by college coaches and pro scouts. Still, coaches must always remember that they're dealing with young people who are emotionally and physically fragile. They are still developing as players and people, so although expectations can justifiably be much higher, it remains important to read the signs of emotional and physical burnout and stress and know when it's necessary to lighten up a bit.

Developing More Than Baseball Players

As players get older, more things compete for their time and attention. High school kids need time for their studies, their social life, and possibly a job. Extracurricular activities and family and outside commitments at school also compete for their attention. Coaches need to be sensitive to all aspects of their players' lives. Yes, it's important for young people to understand what it means to commit to a team and how their decision making can affect the team's chemistry, but it's important to let kids be kids. Part of being a coach is helping to develop well-rounded human beings, so if a player comes to you with a potential conflict, instead of making the kid feel bad or using guilt to force him into honoring a baseball commitment, see if a compromise can be reached that allows him to maximize his experiences. A lesson in compromise can be just as beneficial to a young person as developing an understanding of what it means to make a commitment to a team. And your willingness to work with your players can breed loyalty toward you and help develop an even stronger commitment to the team in the long run.

Working With Parents

Increased parental involvement can make life difficult for coaches at this age group. Your goals and the goals of your players' parents often clash. You're trying to assemble the best team possible to enhance the experience of your players and to bring honor to those who have chosen you to coach. Along the way, you hope to teach your players as much as you can about the game of baseball and any lessons that are transferable from the sport to everyday life. Unfortunately, some parents live vicariously through their children. They hope to relive some unfulfilled glory on the field through their kids and don't want anything to get in the way of that. Thus, at this level open lines of communication between you and parents are as important, or even more important, than with the younger age groups. If you let parents know up front what to expect in terms of your coaching philosophy and how you handle player development and playing time, you'll significantly reduce your number of confrontations. An open line of communication limits, though never eliminates, parental questioning. When dealing with parents, be sure to act professionally, be polite, and don't let your emotions get the best of you.

Older players still must work on the fundamentals every day.

Developing a Flexible Plan

As with the 13-to-14 age group, the basic individual fundamental building blocks should be covered every time your team practices. College and professional players work on fundamentals every day, and your players should, too. Incorporate baserunning, throwing, catching, hitting, and fielding into all of your workouts. All of your team defensive strategies and fundamentals—bunt defenses, first-and-third offenses and defenses, pickoff plays, rundowns, and so on—should be put in place and practiced prior to the start of the season. Accomplish this during practice in the time remaining after the basic fundamentals of throwing, catching, and fielding have been covered.

Once the season begins, there's really no set formula to which you can or should adhere. Beyond the basic individual fundamentals, you'll need to be flexible with your practice plans. Coaches at this level need to be extremely observant. Note mental mistakes and team breakdowns, and design subsequent practices with these in mind. The best time to teach is during practice, so use this time to your full advantage.

Sometimes your team will be executing well as a unit and you might want to plan a fun practice or let them play an intrasquad game. Other times, players might be struggling at the plate, in which case you'll want to use the time normally set aside for team fundamentals to take extra batting practice. Still other times your team may have hit a bump in the road when it comes to the basics of catching and throwing. In that case you might want to spend the team fundamental block reviewing those skills until they are back on track.

Observation is important for coaches during practices, too. There are times when an individual or team fundamental drill has simply gone on too long. The kids are struggling with the execution, losing interest, or both. Practice becomes counterproductive. Good coaches recognize this and move on to something else. There will be future practices in which you can better address the area that's causing problems.

When planning your practices, always keep in mind the goals for this age group as established in chapter 3. These will be your priorities for the season:

1. Throwing mechanics and pitching—long toss; flatwork (drills); continue mastering breaking and off-speed pitches; throwing for accuracy; generating momentum toward the target and following the throw; pickoff mechanics.

2. Hitting—mental aspects (hitter's count versus pitcher's count); two-strike hitting; aggressive versus defensive swings; situational hitting; productive outs; advanced game situations and defenses.

3. Baserunning—one-way leads; going on the first move; reacting to batted balls; tag-up situations; third-base rules; no-out, one-out, and two-out rules.

4. Fielding—understanding and adapting to playing conditions (grass versus dirt, sun, bad fields); fence drill (outfield); crossover and drop steps; do-or-die plays at the plate; preventing runners from taking extra bases; communicating between pitches.

5. Learning team fundamentals—cutoffs and relays (introduce the trailer concept); advanced pickoff plays (daylight play, plays put on by fielders) and when to use them; double plays; advanced game situations and defenses.

These are our recommendations for the 15+ age group:

Practice-to-game ratio: 3 to 1

Length of practices: up to 2 hours or slightly longer (mix in shorter practices when necessary)

Playing time: as equal as possible within the team's accepted goals

Positions: players are more specialized; keep your eyes open for late bloomers.

Base distances: 90 feet

Pitching particulars: kids pitch, but don't let the desire to win cause you to abuse a pitcher's young arm.

Pitching distances: 60 feet, 6 inches

Three-Day Sample Practice Guide

Practice Plan Day 1

5 min.   **Dynamic warm-up**

- Skipping, high-knee skipping, high-knee jogging, bounding, backward running, jogging

5 min.   **Stretching**

- Hamstrings, quads, groin, back, shoulders, triceps

10 min.   **Throwing**

- One-Knee Drill with teammates (early in season)
- Power Position Drill with teammates (early in season)
- Play catch or play Twenty-One with teammates.
- Any throwing or pitching drills from groupings 1, 4, or 5 can be substituted as the season progresses.
- Emphasize long tossing throughout the season.

20 min.   **Infield and outfield work**

- Rolled Ground Balls, Throwing After the Catch Drill, Hitting Ground Balls, Thrown Fly Balls, Rolled or Machine Ground Balls, Hit Fly Balls or Machine Fly Balls

20 min.   **Team fundamentals**

- Choose from cutoffs and relays (introduce trailer), advanced pickoff plays (daylight plays, plays put on by fielders) and situations, advanced game situations (throwing to proper base in certain situations, decoys, and so on), full bunt defenses, pop-up and fly ball priorities, first-and-third offense and defense, and defending steals.

60 min.   **Hitting stations, 15 min. each**

- Soft Toss, Tee Work, Short Toss From the Front, Free Hitting
- Any hitting drill from groupings 1, 4, or 5 can be substituted as the season progresses.
- Infielders and outfielders can take more ground balls and fly balls during this time slot. Pitchers can get in bullpen throwing or do flatwork (pitching or throwing drills from groupings 4 or 5).

10 min.   **Pitcher's fielding practice (PFP) and Big League Baserunning**

- Pitcher Covering First Base Drill, Comebacker Drill, Bunt Drill

Three-Day Sample Practice Guide

Practice Plan Day 2

5 min.   **Dynamic warm-up (same as day 1)**

- Skipping, high-knee skipping, high-knee jogging, bounding, backward running, jogging

5 min.   **Stretching (same as day 1)**

- Hamstrings, quads, groin, back, shoulders, triceps

10 min.   **Throwing**

- One-Knee Drill with teammates (early in season)
- Power Position Drill with teammates (early in season)
- Play catch, play Twenty-One, or long toss with teammates.
- Any throwing or pitching drills from groupings 1, 4, or 5 can be substituted as the season progresses.
- Emphasize long tossing throughout the season.

20 min.   **Infield and outfield work**

- Backhand drills, 4-6/6-4 Drill, First Base Drill, Hitting Ground Balls, Backhand Throwing Drill, Thrown Fly Balls, Rolled or Machine Ground Balls, Hit Fly Balls or Machine Fly Balls, Communication Drill, Crossover Step Drill
- Any infield drill from groupings 1, 4, or 5 can be substituted as the season progresses.

20 min.   **Team fundamentals (same as day 1)**

- Choose from cutoffs and relays (introduce trailer), advanced pick-off plays (daylight plays, plays put on by fielders) and situations, advanced game situations (throwing to proper base in certain situations, decoys, and so on), full bunt defenses, pop-up and fly ball priorities, first-and-third offense and defense, and defending steals.

60 min.   **Hitting stations, 15 min. each**

- Short Toss From the Front, One-Arm Drill, Lob Toss, Stickball Drill, Free Hitting
- Any hitting drill from groupings 1, 4, or 5 can be substituted as the season progresses.
- Infielders and outfielders can take more ground balls and fly balls during this time slot. Pitchers can get in bullpen throwing or do flatwork (pitching or throwing drills from groupings 4 or 5).

10 min.   **Pitchers' fielding practice (PFP) and Big League Baserunning**

- Pitcher Covering First Base Drill, Comebacker Drill, Bunt Drill

(continued)

Three-Day Sample Practice Guide *(continued)*

Practice Plan Day 3

5 min.   **Dynamic warm-up (same as day 1)**

- Skipping, high-knee skipping, high-knee jogging, bounding, backward running, jogging

5 min.   **Stretching (same as day 1)**

- Hamstrings, quads, groin, back, shoulders, triceps

10 min.   **Throwing**

- Play catch, play Twenty-One, or long toss with teammates.
- Other throwing games (optional)
- Any throwing or pitching drills from groupings 1, 4, or 5 can be substituted as the season progresses.
- Emphasize long tossing throughout the season.

20 min.   **Infield and outfield work**

- Box Drill, backhand drills, Hitting Ground Balls, Backhand Throwing Drill, Crossover Step Drill, Drop Step Drill, Pass Patterns, Fence Drill
- Any infield drill from groupings 1, 4, or 5 can be substituted as the season progresses. Drills can be turned into contests on the third or final day of a week.

20 min.   **Team fundamentals (same as day 1)**

- Choose from cutoffs and relays (introduce trailer), advanced pickoff plays (daylight plays, plays put on by fielders) and situations, advanced game situations (throwing to proper base in certain situations, decoys, and so on), full bunt defenses, pop-up and fly ball priorities, first-and-third offense and defense, and defending steals.

60 min.   **Game situations, controlled scrimmage, soft toss game, T-ball game**

10 min.   **Big League Baserunning**

Afterword

Bill Ripken

Keeping It Simple

Our dad, Cal Ripken, Sr., used to say that baseball is a simple game played with bats, balls, and people. Okay, so we've beaten you over the head with that sentiment throughout this book, but that's because we don't want coaches to lose sight of this basic truth. To some, Dad's statement might sound like an oversimplification, but after years of playing the game at the highest level, we couldn't agree more.

If you take a walk to your local park or recreational facility and watch two youth baseball teams preparing for their games, we guarantee you that 99 percent of the time the team that plays catch the best before the game is the one that will win. The better we play catch, the better we play baseball. Even the most complicated plays in baseball, such as the double play, can be broken down into simple parts. When a ground ball is hit to the third baseman with a runner on first, the third baseman must catch the ground ball and then make an accurate throw to the second baseman. The second baseman must catch that throw and then make an accurate throw to the first baseman, who also must catch it. That's it. When broken down, a double play is five simple parts: a catch, a throw, a catch, a throw, and a catch. Five simple parts, but they must be precisely executed in combination to complete the more complicated play. This can't happen if the fundamental building blocks are not in place.

To play baseball effectively, a player must be able to throw the ball, catch the ball, and hit the ball. Sounds easy, right? Well, we all know it's *not* easy. However, from a developmental standpoint, improving should be simple. When it comes to teaching the game, we have developed a philosophy called the Ripken Way. The most important component of the Ripken Way is . . . you guessed it: Keep it simple.

Sometimes, when people spend money to send their children to one of our camps, that one statement, "Keep it simple," causes concern. So many parents these days look at their children, even kids as young as 4 or 5 years old, as future big leaguers. They see baseball as a ticket to fame and fortune, and they want to find that magic potion to make their kids better than everyone else's, whether it's by trying an unproven, gimmicky training aid or searching for some kind of secret approach to help their child hit .400. We live in a world of infomercials and quick fixes. Unfortunately, there are no shortcuts to becoming a better baseball player.

When we say "Keep it simple," all we're saying is that if your 8-year-old catches a ground ball correctly, he's doing it in the exact same way that his favorite professional player does it. The difference is that the pro has done it the right way thousands of times in his life, maybe hundreds of times every day. After your child fields the ball, he should move his feet and throw the ball to first base, just as his favorite player does, although not quite as well. Once again, the pro has made thousands of throws to first base, so his body responds naturally in that situation.

Your child might not stand at home plate the same way his favorite pro stands. The stance is just a starting point, and there are hundreds of acceptable stances in baseball. Certain components of the swing—weight shift, stride, level swing, follow-through—must work together for a hitter to be successful. The same hitting drills we do at camp—Tee Work, Soft Toss, Short Toss, and so on—have been performed by the professional player over and over every day for the better part of his life. He still does them every single day. Every big league hitter does, or he's not a big league hitter for very long.

Practicing the basic fundamentals over and over is the key to becoming a great baseball player. There are no magic shortcuts or products to enhance a player's chances of playing at the highest level. The only way to make it to the big leagues is through hard work and repetition of the fundamental building blocks until the routine plays become truly routine.

You don't learn to make great plays or handle bad hops by practicing diving stops or taking ground balls on a bad field. Similarly, you don't learn to hit breaking balls and off-speed pitches by hitting a steady diet of curveballs and change-ups. Once you have developed your muscle memory to the point that the fundamental movements become second nature—so that you don't have to think even for a split-second when catching a routine ground ball or hitting a fast-ball— your body will automatically learn to adapt to the nonroutine plays and the tricky pitches.

The game of baseball becomes complicated fast enough. There's no reason to complicate it more. If we give a young player too much to think about during a game, the result can be paralysis. Instead of reacting naturally to a batted or pitched ball, he or she thinks of all the possibilities and then can't function to the best of his or her ability.

Catch the ball and throw the ball. See the ball and hit the ball. When Dad coached third base for the Orioles, he would frequently yell, "See the ball come up to home plate and hit it." That was his way of trying to relax the hitter. Don't overcomplicate. See the ball and hit it.

The time to give a player advice about his swing is not during a game, when the pitcher is throwing as hard as he can and trying to trick the hitter by making the ball move all over the place. No, the time for advice is when players are performing hitting drills in practice. Each simple drill can help a hitter develop one part of his or her swing to the point that the body performs that portion of the swing automatically come game time.

For example, when players at our camps hit off a batting tee, all we want them to focus on is their weight shift. We tell them that to generate more power they have to "Go back to go forward." That's all we talk about when it comes to tee work. For soft toss, the catch phrase is "Loose hands, quick bat." Gripping the bat loosely in the fingers allows the wrists to unlock and creates more bat speed. When we do short toss from the front, we toss the ball to the outside part of the plate and direct players to "Use the big part of the field." We want them to keep the front shoulder in, stride toward the pitcher, and hit a hard line drive.

Players do drills at a pace much slower than game speed and with nothing on the line. This allows coaches to suggest corrections and adjustments that can be practiced and perfected without worrying about a game situation or a pitcher with a mystifying breaking ball. Once each individual drill is ingrained in a hitter, adjusting during a game becomes much easier. All of the simple, individual components fall into place and allow the hitter to develop an effective swing.

Hitting drills also can be used to troubleshoot. When a coach notices a player doing something wrong at the plate during a game, he can make a note of it and find a drill to correct the problem at the next practice.

When it comes to fielding, we rarely hit a ground ball during our camps. By rolling ground balls over flat surfaces to players, we can control the speed and the hops, allowing players to learn how to field properly without worrying about taking a ball off the lip or nose. Once players feel confident in fielding ground balls the right way, they'll automatically do it in games. If a player gets in proper fielding position every time during a game, he's much more likely to be able to handle a bad hop or make an extraordinary play than a player who has not developed the proper fundamental base. We have used this teaching method with players of all age levels, including college players, and we've had great success. This is not to say that coaches should never hit ground balls to their players. But we suggest allowing players to become extremely comfortable fielding ground balls before you hit balls at them.

Can repetition of the basic fundamentals become boring for kids? Sure. That's where a coach's creativity comes into play. Turn simple drills into contests. Encourage players on your team to compete against one another. Have players shoot for "world record" scores in every drill. Competition increases focus and maintains interest. If you put your mind to it, you can make your drills so much fun that you have to force your players to stop practicing.

"Keep it simple" doesn't mean that our method of teaching is too elementary for advanced players. It only means that by practicing the fundamental skills over and over, players will naturally develop the comfort level, ability, and muscle memory they need to make difficult and complicated plays. If this method is good enough for the pros, it's good enough for the kids on your travel team or in your high school program, too.

Remember what Dad used to say: "Practice doesn't make perfect. *Perfect* practice makes perfect." It's human nature to complicate things. Coaches often want to combine two or three drills into one. They want to come up with flashy ways to warm up in hopes of intimidating the opposing team. Keep in mind that the more complicated you make things, the more likely you are to confuse your players or create situations they can't handle. A complicated drill with several parts that incorporates multiple fundamentals might make it difficult for your players to execute any one part of the drill effectively. This means they're not developing any specific fundamental skill to the fullest. Breaking the complicated play down into its fundamental elements and working hard to perfect each element before combining them into one complete action is the best way to facilitate "perfect" practice.

Coaches who are unable to explain why their players should do something a certain way are less likely to get their message across. You don't know how many times I hear at camp, "My dad says I should do it this way." Well, if I can show players the *proper* way to perform a skill and then tell them why they should do it that way, they are much more likely to attempt the proper method. If I just shoot back a knee-jerk reply like "Do it my way because I said so," those kids are likely to revert back to their father's way as soon as they're out of my sight.

The last two elements of our philosophy—"celebrate the individual" and "make it fun"—are aimed at keeping young players interested in the game. If you look around the sporting landscape, other sports promote the individual styles that players bring to the contests. This is attractive to young people. The Major League baseball season is 162 games long, so some of the enthusiasm you see on the field early in the season or during the postseason isn't always present during the dog days of August. Maintaining an even keel mentally is important for big league players, but unfortunately that sometimes makes the game seem dull to some people. We want our kids to let their personalities and excitement show on the baseball field.

Many baseball instructors are set in their ways. They teach that their way of approaching the game or a specific skill is the only way, almost as if they're trying to clone young players. Baseball is very much a mental game and a game of adjustments. There are deceptive pitches, bad-hop ground balls, and wind-blown fly balls. Baseball is also an individual team game in which each player must execute his or her

Make it fun to keep kids interested in the game.

individual assignment for the good of the team as a whole. Every time a pitcher throws a pitch, every time a batter stands in the box, and every time a ball is hit at a fielder, the player involved in the play is under pressure to perform. A player must be relaxed and comfortable enough to make the necessary adjustments and handle the pressure. Players who aren't comfortable with a particular approach and are simply trying to please their coaches are going to be less successful than players who are relaxed and familiar with what they're trying to do.

Yes, certain fundamental approaches are necessary in the game of baseball, but there's a lot of room to let players be themselves and stay within their comfort zones while playing the game. Every player doesn't have to stand the same way at home plate. Every ready position doesn't have to be exactly the same. Every throwing motion cannot be identical. One of the most important aspects of coaching is the ability to observe a player's results before tinkering with his or her approach. Let players be themselves.

Finally, making the game fun is extremely important to the health of the sport. Kids love to play games. That's a fact. As long as they are getting the opportunity to play, they're going to be happy to a point. But a group of kids can play 100 games, and if they lose all of them or aren't competitive in most of them, that's not going to make for a fun season. The happiness they felt in game 1 is going to disappear by game 10. Kids are sponges. They have a thirst for learning and improving. Getting better is fun. But kids won't get better if they don't practice.

As we've shown you in this book, practice can be as much fun as real games. If your league plays only games, with no practices, please approach the commissioner or board of directors and explain the importance of practice. If you are told that kids won't have as much fun practicing as they do playing games, suggest that you can prove them all wrong. If they won't change their minds, find an open field and hold practice there. We've given you enough options to run a practice almost anywhere.

You have seen the reasons behind our instructional philosophy, but, once again, everything starts with keeping it simple. Let common sense prevail. On the field, design simple practices that are fast paced, that keep your players moving, and that can be done in small groups. Provide a safe, comfortable environment. If kids get bored, turn a drill into a contest. Teach simple fundamental building blocks that once perfected can be combined to execute complicated plays. Speak to the kids in simple terms; demonstrate skills so they understand them. Don't try to do too much teaching during games or while players are in the process of hitting or pitching. Use practice time to dissect mistakes or problem areas that you've noticed during games. Keep the five simple goals for your age group in mind, and if your team accomplishes them, consider yourself a successful coach.

Off the field, the formula for being a successful coach is just as simple. Be a positive role model. Explain your methods and philosophies. Be organized. Keep the lines of communication open throughout the season. Be polite, professional, and courteous. Maintain an even temperament during games and practices and when dealing with players or parents. Make sure that you enjoy yourself and that everyone involved with the team feels your excitement and enthusiasm for the game.

Nothing is more rewarding than seeing a group of young people you have coached improve and enjoy themselves. Too many coaches are frustrated by a lack of knowledge and a lack of resources. We hope that the methods and the information presented in this book help make your coaching experience rewarding. We hope you can develop in your players the passion we share for the game of baseball, because the future of our game depends on our ability to excite the young people of today about this wonderful sport.

Appendix

John Habyan

Working Pitchers In

A dilemma that faces baseball coaches at virtually every level is how to make sure that pitchers who play other positions are able to get their mound throwing, running, and flatwork in during practices (we'll explain "flatwork" in a few minutes). In fact, depending on the number of catchers and coaches a team has, it might be a challenge to figure out when to get any of a team's pitchers the work they need between appearances.

It can be extremely difficult to balance the work that pitchers who play other positions need between outings with the amount of throwing they should do if they hope to stay sharp at their other positions. It also can be tough to find the time in practice to allow your pitchers to get their throwing in, to hit, and to work on their individual defense. We hope some of these ideas will help.

Plan an Effective Practice

A coach's ability to be organized and plan an effective practice will allow him or her to accomplish all of his or her coaching goals on a consistent basis. This includes finding time for pitchers who play other positions to work on all of the fundamental skills they need to be successful.

Start by having your players perform a dynamic warm-up that gets their hearts pumping and allows them to stretch and throw for up to 20 minutes. After that, I usually spend about 20 minutes on infield and outfield fungos with players throwing from their positions for part of that time (without overdoing it).

From there we move into team fundamentals. It's important to cover at least one, if not two, team fundamentals every day in practice.

These fundamentals include baserunning, cutoffs and relays, pickoffs and rundowns, bunt defenses, and first-and-third defenses. Some days are better than others when it comes to fundamentals. If kids don't understand the concepts after 20 minutes, they probably aren't going to get them at all that day, so we move on to something else. We'll return to the problem area at another practice session.

After fundamentals comes batting practice. This is your opportunity to make the best use of your time, not only for your hitters but for your pitchers as well.

BP Is More Than Just Batting Practice

An effective batting practice is more than just one player hitting and everyone else watching. By using small groups and breaking batting practice down into stations lasting no more than 10 to 15 minutes each, the process becomes much more efficient and prevents boredom from setting in. Plus, doing this allows your pitchers to get their work in.

Dedicate one station to fundamental hitting drills: Tee Work, Soft Toss, Short Toss, or another drill or a combination of drills. In another station work on live hitting and baserunning on the field. There might be two fielding stations, one in the infield and one in the outfield, at which players field the balls hit during batting practice without making throws to bases. Between pitches, a coach can hit players infield and outfield fungos to keep kids interested and allow them to work on individual defensive fundamentals.

Group pitchers and catchers together so that pitchers can get their throwing in during the fielding stations. The amount of throwing and the type of throwing that needs to be done depends on the pitcher. At the high school and youth levels, most starting pitchers get one starting assignment a week. If this is the case, they should throw a bullpen session either two or three days after their start. If they start once a week, it's probably okay to wait until the third day for their bullpen session. If they're getting two starts in a week, it might be a better idea to schedule the bullpen session for the second day.

Defining a Bullpen Session

In reference to pitchers, you sometimes hear coaches say, "He needs to throw a bullpen." All this means is that pitchers throw from a mound at the regulation distance (for the player's age) and at maximum velocity for a pre-determined amount of time or a pre-determined number of pitches. The focus should be on fastballs and location, but some pitchers should also throw a set number of other pitches *if* they throw these pitches in games. In general, younger pitchers should be throwing almost all fastballs to help build arm strength. They should be introduced to off-speed and breaking pitches only as they approach physical maturity, and even then the use of these pitches should be monitored closely by a coach.

How long should a bullpen session last? This is where things get tricky. If a pitcher is only a pitcher and doesn't play another position, the bullpen session should last about 15 minutes. For players who play other positions, you need to adjust accordingly. A pitcher who's the starting shortstop, for instance, should probably throw for about 8 to 10 minutes. The amount a reliever throws between appearances will depend on how much work he's getting. A pitcher who's being used out of the bullpen frequently might not need a bullpen session at all. If your starters are getting the job done in games, you might want to have your reliever throw a full bullpen. A pitcher who has been used only occasionally might need to be scaled down to 8 or 10 minutes, or even less. Common sense should prevail here.

The bullpen session is not designed for the pitcher to work on problem areas. This session is part of the rehabilitation process after throwing in a game to help maintain shoulder conditioning. That's why it's imperative that the pitcher focuses on throwing and locating mostly fastballs. The pitcher must get his work in without worrying about why his curveball is hanging or why his change-up is staying up in the strike zone. Throwing every type of pitch from a mound is important to help pitchers stay sharp, but fastballs should be the main area of concentration.

Drills and Flatwork

I don't intend to go into specifics about throwing programs, running programs, or flatwork at this point. What I want to do here is demonstrate how to fit your pitchers' extra work into the framework of an organized practice and the best way to handle pitchers who play other positions.

If a pitcher is struggling with mechanics, control, or a specific pitch, he can try to make corrections during the fielding stations at practice. This is called "flatwork" because it's done from a shortened distance on flat ground, not from a mound. Long tossing can also be incorporated

Batting practice offers coaches an oppertunity to work with their pitchers more closely.

into this portion of practice. Many of the drills described in chapter 5 can be performed during flatwork. Most flatwork is done from about 40 feet or so, and pitchers can work in pairs to make even better use of their time. Fielding stations also afford pitchers an opportunity to do their running and conditioning. If a pitcher is also an infielder, make sure that player gets his or her throwing or running in during the outfield fielding station. The opposite is true for pitchers who also are outfielders. This allows them to make the best use of their time.

Pitcher's Fielding Practice

When it comes to pitchers, there's one last fundamental that should always be addressed but that's often overlooked: pitcher's fielding practice (PFP). At some point during every practice pitchers should work on fielding comebackers, fielding bunts, and covering first base on balls to the right side. Once again, fitting PFP into the framework of a practice can be difficult. I've found that spending 10 to 15 minutes on PFP after every practice is the best way to go. PFP sometimes can be addressed when hitting fungos at the beginning of practice, but once again, you run into the problem of how to handle pitchers who play other positions.

Additional Ripken Resources

Ripken Baseball is committed to growing the game of baseball worldwide the Ripken Way. The following products provide players, parents, and coaches with more detailed information about how to play and practice the game the right way. Additional information is available at www.ripkenbaseball.com.

Books

Play Baseball the Ripken Way: The Complete Illustrated Guide to the Fundamentals by Cal Ripken, Jr. and Bill Ripken with Larry Burke; Random House, 2004. Available at www.ripkenbaseball.com.

Parenting Young Athletes the Ripken Way: Ensuring the Best Experiences for Your Kids in Any Sport by Cal Ripken, Jr., with Rick Wulf; Penguin, 2006. Available at www.ripkenbaseball.com.

Get in the Game: 8 Principles of Perseverance That Make the Difference by Cal Ripken, Jr., with Donald T. Phillips; Penguin, 2007. Available in 2007.

Instructional Products

Playing Baseball the Ripken Way DVD Series; available at www.ripkenbaseball.com

> *Playing Defense the Ripken Way,* 2005, approximately 60 minutes
> *Pitching the Ripken Way,* 2005, approximately 60 minutes
> *Hitting the Ripken Way,* 2005, approximately 60 minutes

Teaching Baseball the Ripken Way: A Coaches' Clinic with Cal and Bill Ripken CD-ROM; includes nearly two hours of instructional video for hitting, pitching, playing infield, and playing outfield as well as more than 50 pages of printable lessons. Available at www.ripkenbaseball.com.

Ripken Quickball

Ripken Quickball is both an innovative backyard game and a great tool for training. The durable plastic balls can be used to perform virtually any of our hitting drills, to play an exciting and quick version of baseball, or to permit batting practice when space is limited.

Ripken Quickball Hitting Set; includes 1 bat, 6 balls, instructional game booklet, and clamshell packaged for hanging.

Ripken Quickball Bucket of Balls; includes 24 patented Quickballs in a bucket perfect for transport and storage.

Ripken Quickball Game Bucket; includes a bucket of 30 game balls, 1 set rubber throw-down bases, 2 scoring buckets, 1 foam batting tee, 1 AutoUmp strikezone target, 1 stopwatch, 1 programming DVD, 1 illustrated program guide, 5 20 × 30 fence markers, 12 field cones, 2 plastic bats; send a note to usaquickball@aol.com or call (336) 655-7275 for more information.

Ripken Quickball QuickRip Bat (available in 2007); includes Quickballs and a shaved-down, hard plastic stickball-type bat.

The Jugs Company

Known worldwide for its pitching machine, the Jugs Company has developed a complete line of innovative products that aid with baseball instruction and training. You will find several Jugs products useful as you implement many of the drills found in this book. You can see the products firsthand at www.jkpsports.com and www.ripkenbaseball.com.

The Jugs Company has several types of batting tees, screens, nets, dimple balls, machine-friendly baseballs, plastic balls, portable batting cages, and batting cage netting, among other products. Many products can be bought in combination (toss machines, balls, and instant screens, for example) at a discounted price.

Hardball Pitching Machines

Smaller, inexpensive models for youth league players are available. Baseball/softball combination machines, one-wheel machines, and two-wheel curveball models are also available.

Lite Flite Machines

The Lite Flite Machine allows teams to take batting practice virtually anywhere, indoors or outdoors. The Lite Flite machine throws soft, yellow Lite Flite Balls at challenging, but not overwhelming, speeds. The machine is great for batting practice and fun defensive drills.

Lite Flite Balls

Lite Flite Balls are soft, sponge rubber yellow baseballs with raised seams that can be used with the Lite Flite Machine or separately. They are great for working with younger players and can be used for fun drills with older players, too. Lite Flite balls also are great for impromptu batting practice or drill work when space is limited or hitting screens are not available.

Instant Screens

Instant Screens are portable pop-up screens that are ideal for hitting drills at home, on the road, or even in the backyard. The screens have a built-in red target that also makes them excellent for drills that focus on throwing accuracy.

Toss Machines

The Jugs Toss Machine holds a dozen baseballs or dimple balls, is battery operated and easily portable, and throws perfect soft-toss strikes every time. This machine is a must when coaches or other volunteers are at a premium.

Index

About the Authors

Cal Ripken, Jr., is baseball's all-time Iron Man. He retired from baseball in October 2001 after 21 seasons with the Baltimore Orioles. His name appears in the record books repeatedly, most notably as one of only eight players in history to record more than 400 home runs and 3,000 hits. In 1995, Ripken broke Lou Gehrig's record for consecutive games played (2,130) and voluntarily ended his streak in 1998 after playing in a world-record 2,632 consecutive games.

Among his other on-field accolades are American League Rookie of the Year (1982), two-time American League Most Valuable Player (1983, 1991), two-time Gold Glove recipient (1991, 1992), two-time All-Star Game MVP (1991, 2001), and 19 All-Star Game selections. He also was named to Major League Baseball's All-Century Team in 1999.

Ripken has made a tremendous impact on the sport and on fans everywhere. In 1999, Babe Ruth League, Inc., changed the name of its largest division (5- to 12-year-olds) from Bambino to Cal Ripken Baseball. More than 700,000 youths play Cal Ripken Baseball worldwide. He is using the platform that baseball has provided him to construct a baseball complex in his hometown of Aberdeen, Maryland. The one-of-a-kind facility consists of Ripken Stadium, a state-of-the-art 6,000-seat minor league ballpark that is home to the hugely successful Class A Aberdeen IronBirds. Adjacent to the minor league ballpark is the Ripken Youth Baseball Academy, consisting of eight youth fields, including a youth-sized replica of Oriole Park at Camden Yards, a synthetic training infield, a bullpen area, and batting cages.

Ripken resides in Maryland with his wife, Kelly, and their children, Rachel and Ryan.

Bill Ripken, a 12-year Major League veteran, began his career with the Baltimore Orioles in 1987 under the direction of his father, Cal Ripken, Sr., and alongside brother Cal Ripken, Jr. This was the first and remains the only time in Major League Baseball history that a father simultaneously managed two of his sons.

After five and a half seasons with the Orioles, Ripken, who would later return to Baltimore for a year, played for Texas, Cleveland, and Detroit. In 1988, he was second among American League second basemen in double plays turned (100). At the plate, Ripken led the Baltimore Orioles in hitting with a .291 average and 28 doubles in 1990. Ripken, a second baseman by trade, had a fielding percentage of .9927 in 1992, the best of any Major League second baseman that season, and his career fielding percentage at second base (.987) ranks among baseball's all-time leaders. One of the top-rated second basemen in baseball history, Ripken was voted by his peers as one of the players most likely to manage a big league team.

Ripken is the co-owner and executive vice president of Ripken Baseball Inc., a sales and marketing company founded in 1999 and based in Baltimore. Ripken is involved in all aspects of the business and regularly instructs at youth camps and coaching clinics. Through his work with these programs, he has become recognized as one of America's premiere baseball instructors. Ripken also is involved in the continued development of the Ripken Academy in Aberdeen, Maryland, and the management of Ripken Baseball's minor league teams in Aberdeen and Augusta, Georgia.

Ripken lives in Fallston, Maryland, with his wife, Candace, and his children, Miranda, Anna, Reese, and Jack.

Scott Lowe joined Ripken Baseball in 1999 after eight years working in college sports publicity. Lowe initially served as the general manager of the company's camps and clinics division, developing Ripken Baseball's youth camps, coaching clinics, and other instructional programs. Presently he writes and designs Ripken Baseball's *Coach's Clipboard* e-newsletter, which is distributed to amateur baseball coaches around the world on a monthly basis. He also oversees the creation and distribution of Ripken Baseball instructional products and is involved in the development and implementation of the company's coaching education and other baseball instructional programs.

After graduating summa cum laude from the University of Maryland College of Journalism in 1991, Lowe spent two years as an athletic communications assistant at Princeton University. He was the assistant director of sports information and served as the athletics marketing coordinator at Drexel University in Philadelphia from 1993 to 1995 before returning to the Baltimore area to become the assistant director of athletic communications at Loyola College. Lowe served in that capacity before being promoted to the position of head sports information director in 1997. Lowe left Loyola in 1998 to form his own baseball camp business prior to joining Ripken Baseball in September 1999.

In addition to his full-time position at Ripken Baseball, he has served for three years as the head coach of varsity baseball at the Park School in Baltimore, compiling a 45–19 record and leading the Bruins to three consecutive MIAA B Conference playoff appearances, including a trip to the 2006 championship game, after the school had failed to reach the postseason the previous seven years.

Lowe resides in Owings Mills, Maryland, with his wife, Robin, and children, Devin and Sydney.

"I couldn't be more excited that Ripken Baseball is partnering with the Babe Ruth League and the American Sport Education Program to develop an online coaching education program for the nearly 200,000 volunteer coaches in all divisions of Babe Ruth Baseball and Softball.

This partnership will allow us to arm even more coaches with the resources that they need to make the game better for even more youth baseball players."

Cal Ripken, Jr.
President/CEO
Ripken Baseball Inc.

BABE RUTH LEAGUE COACHING EDUCATION CENTER
POWERED BY RIPKEN BASEBALL

With the requirement that all baseball and softball coaches affiliated with Babe Ruth League, Inc. and Ripken Baseball, Inc. become **certified by July 31, 2008**, this website makes it easy for you to gain your certification quickly and effectively through the convenience of online learning.

Register for your course today!

www.BabeRuthCoaching.org • www.RipkenCoaching.org